I0832810

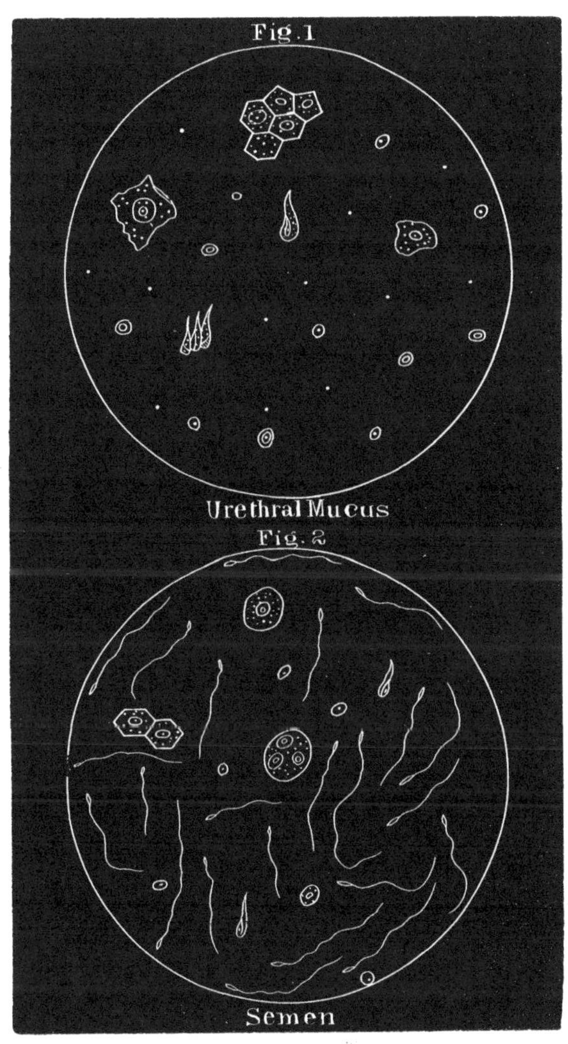
Fig. 1
Urethral Mucus
Fig. 2
Semen

SPERMATORRHŒA:

ITS CAUSES,

SYMPTOMS, RESULTS, AND TREATMENT.

BY

ROBERTS BARTHOLOW, A.M., M.D.,

Professor of Materia Medica and Therapeutics in the Medical College of Ohio; Lecturer on Clinical Medicine, and Physician to the Hospital of the Good Samaritan; Lecturer on Morbid Anatomy, and Pathologist to the Cincinnati Hospital, &c.

THIRD EDITION, REVISED.

NEW YORK:
WILLIAM WOOD & CO., 61 WALKER STREET.
1871.

TABLE OF CONTENTS.

PREFACE TO THE FIRST EDITION.

A SHORT essay on the Pathology and Treatment of Spermatorrhœa, based upon a clinical lecture delivered at St. John's Hospital, and published in the *Cincinnati Journal of Medicine*, having met with a very favorable reception from the profession, it has seemed desirable to give the subject fuller treatment from the same point of view.

There have been but few special treatises on this disease of a reputable character. The work of Lallemand, *Des pertes séminales involontaires*, Paris et Montpelier, 1837–41, is the source from which subsequent writers have drawn their information. A portion of this work has been presented in an English dress by two translators—Wood and McDougall. Additions to the translation of the last named have been made by Maris Wilson, and in this form it is the principal authority now in the hands of American physicians. The subject is also discussed, necessarily in an incomplete manner, in various works on the practice of medicine and surgery. Besides these authorities, Mr. Acton has lately addressed the general public in a work on the reproductive organs, in which he discourses more or less fully on Spermatorrhœa.

I think it is a reproach to our profession that this subject has been permitted, in a measure by our own indifference, to pass into the hands of the unscrupulous pretenders, whose suggestive publications are amongst the crying evils of our time. Because the subject is disagreeable, and to a certain degree disreputable, competent physicians are loath to be concerned with it. The same unnecessary fastidiousness causes the treatment of this malady to be avoided in private practice; and the unfortunate patients, thus precluded from obtaining intelligent advice, fall into the hands of advertising specialists, who excite their worst apprehensions for a mercenary purpose. For this reason, and to obviate the sad consequences which result from spermatorrhœa, it is our duty to exert our best efforts in behalf of those afflicted with this malady. We should endeavor to attain to correct views of its pathology, and apply our knowledge to its cure—if for no other reason, for the good of our species.

My little work will have done all that I can desire for it, if it assist the practitioner in forming correct views of the nature of spermatorrhœa, and enable him to conduct cases of this disease to a more successful issue than he has hitherto been able to accomplish.

PREFACE TO THE SECOND EDITION.

A SECOND edition of this monograph having been called for within less than a year after the publication of the first, is a gratifying evidence of the appreciation of my labor by the medical profession.

In the present edition, some typographical errors, overlooked in the first, have been corrected; a table of contents has been appended, and new matter has been added at various places throughout the volume. These improvements will, I trust, make the present edition still more worthy of the favor so largely accorded to the first.

PREFACE TO THE THIRD EDITION.

I HAVE to express my acknowledgments to the medical profession for the very great favor with which the two previous editions of this work have been received. As it now appears in this edition, the material has been rearranged, and in large part rewritten. Some illustrations have been introduced, and an appendix of formulæ added. The value of the book will, I trust, be considered to be enhanced by these changes and additions.

More enlarged experience since the appearance of the first edition, has not caused me to amend any of my views of the nature and true mode of treating spermatorrhœa. I am, indeed, more than ever confirmed in the view that it is a *neurosis*, and that the treatment, to be successful, must be founded on this pathological basis.

R. B.

27 WEST 8TH STREET, CINCINNATI, OHIO.

NOTICES OF THE FIRST EDITION OF THIS WORK.

From the New York Medical Journal for October, 1866.

"Lallemand's erroneous teachings on the Pathology and Treatment of Spermatorrhœa have been, for more than twenty years, the guide of the majority of practitioners, and we are glad, at length, to see the subject ably and judiciously discussed in a special treatise, and the more correct views of modern investigators fully set forth. Viewed in this respect alone, the little work before us will accomplish a good purpose; but again it will be productive of a double good, for an enlightened comprehension of the subject will lessen that aversion which too many practitioners entertain toward a subject at once disagreeable in itself, and to a certain extent disreputable, and thus many an unfortunate and truly pitiable subject of this distressing malady will be rescued from the hands of the ignorant and pretending charlatans to whose mercenary offers he is not unfrequently driven in desperation to resort by the indifference of the regular practitioner. The book supplies a want that has long been felt by the profession, and can be confidently recommended as a reliable guide to both student and practitioner, and as embracing the more recent and well-sustained advances that have been made, both in the pathology and therapeutics of the malady in question."

From the Medical Record, November 1, 1866.

"This duodecimo, which is a philosophical revision of a by no means generally understood subject, clears away much of the rubbish that has heretofore encumbered its literature. The writer, who substitutes for many of the vexed questions very tenable views of his own, makes no violent deductions, but states objections with candor, and arrives at his conclusions by logical sequences. We bespeak for the work a cordial reception on the part of the profession, and for the author additional laurels to a growing reputation."

From the Twenty-fourth Annual Report of the Managers of the State Lunatic Asylum, Utica, N. Y., for the year 1866.

Report of Dr. Gray, Superintendent, p. 33:

"I would commend to the attention of the profession the admirable little work of Dr. Roberts Bartholow on Spermatorrhœa, recently published be Wm. Wood & Co., New York."

NOTICES.

From the Boston Medical and Surgical Journal, November 8, 1866.

"This little book is a well-written and judicious essay on Spermatorrhœa considered under the above divisions, which we can recommend to the perusal of our readers. The valuable and practical instruction on treatment it contains will be found worthy of careful stndy by all who are consulted upon this neglected affection."

From the Philadelphia Medical and Surgical Reporter, Sept. 15, 1866.

"Dr. Bartholow's treatise upon Spermatorrhœa seems to us to have been judiciously conceived and well executed. Lallemand's ideas of the pathology and treatment of this affection have too long maintained the sway of routine. Central in those ideas, as all know, is that of the constant importance, in the production of Spermatorrhœa, of irritation or inflammation of the prostatic portion of the urethra, and of the seminal ducts. Hence his use of the *porte-caustique.*

". Dr. Bartholow summarily disposes of all this, and asserts, we believe truly that the affection in question should take its place among the *neuroses*, as essentially a functional derangement of the excito-motor spinal system. He would limit the use of the porte-caustique to those conditions of inflammation ulceration, and hyperæsthesia of the prostatic portion of the urethra, really proved to exist, and refractory to other less painful and dangerous methods ; or, for moral effect, to obstinate cases accompanied by severe hypochondria, or continued masturbation. Moral treatment of a larger kind, with appropriate regimen, tonics, etc., will be of service in the greater number of cases. *Circumcision*, it is well urged, should not be omitted in two classes of cases : 1. Those in which the habit of masturbation is due to the hyperæsthesia of the glans, produced by an elongated prepuce, and the irritation of retained sebaceous matter. 2. Those in which the same cause (a peripheral irritation) induces the venereal orgasm and involuntary discharge.

"This treatise, however, goes very systematically over the whole subject. It is extremely well worth reading by all practitioners, as a good exposition of sound views. We will only mention, as particularly of interest, in addition to what has been said—the denial by Dr. Bartholow of the frequency of ulceration or inflammation of the prostatic portion of the urethra in spermatorrhœa, in this country, at least; his clear discrimination between the not uncommon mucous discharges and true diurnal seminal pollutions; and his testimony to the positively anaphrodisiac effects of bromide of potassium in appropriate cases. This remedy, he states, 'will be effectual in proportion to the degree in which structural lesions are absent, or in other words, in proportion to the degree in which these morbid states are functional rather than organic.' The failures of Dr. S. W. D. Williams and others, are accounted for by the existence of organic causes."

SPERMATORRHŒA:

ITS CAUSES, SYMPTOMS, RESULTS, AND TREATMENT.

INTRODUCTION.

It seems to be necessary to define, at the outset, what is meant by *Spermatorrhœa.* The sense in which this term is used not always being the same, confusion has arisen as to its real pathological import. By some, following in a literal sense its etymological signification, this term is restricted to that condition in which there is a constant stillicidium of semen, without, of course, the preliminary phenomena of erection and ejaculation. If this definition be accepted, spermatorrhœa can be admitted to exist but rarely.

According to a more widely received view, spermatorrhœa consists in the emission of semen without copulation, or in involuntary seminal losses of every kind. If the former definition be defective by reason of too limited scope, the latter is defective in a more injurious degree, because it embraces a physiological as well as a pathological state.

The term *spermatorrhœa* should be restricted to that condition in which involuntary seminal losses occur with sufficient frequency to produce a definite morbid state.

It is very important to be accurate on this point, for nothing is more common than mistaken views in regard to the pathological importance of occasional spermal losses. A physiological condition is frequently confounded with the results of disease. The prevalence of this error is due chiefly to the false statements so persistently put forth by advertising specialists in regard to the evil consequences of nocturnal pollutions. I cannot too strongly impress on my readers, that after the period of puberty involuntary seminal losses occur in the continent with more or less frequency, according to the activity of their sexual organs. The young man who, ignorant of its nature, happens to this accident for the first time, is much concerned, especially if he have read the impure publications on this topic now so widely distributed. In such a case the intelligent and humane physician may render a lasting service by an exact statement of the importance of these physiological emissions.

Although many cases of so-called spermatorrhœa are physiological in character, we should not therefore assume that no morbid state is produced by frequent involuntary losses.

Spermatorrhœa is also a symptom of lesion of some part of the central nervous system. It has, then, but little importance as compared with the serious disease of which it is but an indication.

It follows from the foregoing considerations, in order to have a true comprehension of spermatorrhœa, it must be studied from several points of view. I purpose, therefore, to treat of the subject according to the following scheme:

1. True Spermatorrhœa.
    - Its Causes.
        - Physical.
        - Moral.
    - Its Symptoms.
    - Its Results.
2. Spermatorrhœa as a Symptom.
3. False or Imaginary Spermatorrhœa.
4. Treatment.

I.

TRUE SPERMATORRHŒA.

CAUSES.

Physical.—The vice of masturbation is undoubtedly the chief cause. The growth of the sexual apparatus at the period of puberty is accompanied by abundant secretion of the seminal fluid, which accumulates in the reservoirs. The sexual instinct, then fully developed, exerts a powerful influence over the mind, whilst the reason is not in a sufficiently matured state to correct the *mirages* of the imagination. An accidental friction of the erect organ in these moments of delirium makes the unfortunate youth acquainted with a new and voluptuous sensation.* Ignorant of the dreadful consequences which must ensue from the repeated perpetration of this act, the youth perseveres in his secret pleasures until arrested by realizing some of the sad effects upon the mind and body which follow.

* *Tissot. L'Onanisme. Dissertation sur les Maladies produites par la Masturbation.* Also, *Fournier et Begin, Dictionnaire des Sciences Médicales*, vol. xxxi., pp. 100–134.

Although the practice of this vice is not confined to boys of the nervous type, yet it finds in them victims the most willing, and the least able to resist the continually increasing demands of the habit. Boys of vigorous constitution, in whom the digestive and muscular systems are well developed, are less under the control of these erotic impulses, and are more able to resist the inroads of the habit when formed, because in them the exercises of youth and the satisfaction of the appetite occupy their minds.

A premature and unnatural development of the genital apparatus may give origin to the vice of masturbation. Mr. South has related an extraordinary case of premature puberty, in which involuntary losses occurred:—

"When he was about four months old, the hair on the pubes began to grow very thickly and black, at which time the penis increased in size, particularly the glans, so that it gradually extended beyond the prepuce, till about fifteen months, when it was entirely exposed; the pubes were then completely covered with black, curling hair. . . . . Soon after this, she (his mother) noticed that his linen was stained two or three times in the week. . . . . She also states that since he has been in town (six weeks) the emissions have been more frequent than for some time previously."* Mr. South gives the following measurements of the penis of this extraordinary infant: length of penis when pendent from the symphysis pubis, three inches; length of penis when erect, six inches. This is probably the "most rare and curious" case of premature puberty on record; certainly it is the earliest period at which spermatorrhœa has occurred. Such an instance is wholly exceptional. Nevertheless, a premature development of the sexual organs may constitute an occasional cause of self-pollution—the more especially if such development be not accompanied by corresponding growth of the other organs and systems of the body, and of the reason and moral control.

Independently, however, of a premature development of the sexual apparatus, the vice of masturbation may be contracted at a very tender age, a very instructive example of which has been narrated by Mr. Heckford. "I believe it is not

* Medico-Chirurgical Transactions, vol. xii., p. 76.

generally known," says Mr. Heckford, "that this vice is practised not only by adults of both sexes, but also by young children, and even infants in the cradle. The following notes, kindly given me by Dr. Hughlings Jackson, are a sufficient guarantee as to the correctness of this assertion, at least as regards one case. . . . The following is the narrative of Dr. Jackson :—A woman came to the Hospital for Epilepsy and Paralysis, on account of fits. She took the opportunity of asking my advice about her child. The boy was fifteen months old; he was delicate, and had never been able to stand; but the special circumstance about which the mother wished to hear my opinion was the peculiar position of his legs. The right leg was almost always placed high up over the other, and he kept it moving in a sawing way towards the pelvis. The penis was in the way of friction, and was quite stiff when I examined it. He was much annoyed at my interference with the movements of his leg, making resistance and crying. . . . The boy had congenital phymosis, but he did not cry when he made water. Mr. Hutchison was kind enough, at my request, to circumcise him. . . . After this the habit ceased, for a time at least, and the child much improved in health." *

I have had lately under observation a case, a boy four years of age, who had practised the habit for two years. He exposed the penis to friction between the thigh and abdomen. His mother informed me that he was much excited during the act, and at its termination passed into a nervous state, preceded by a shudder. He had frequent epileptic convulsions. Circumcision, although it interrupted, did not cure the habit, for the boy resumed it again after the wound healed. Threats, punishment, and restraint were alike unavailing to prevent the perpetration of the act.

A very influential cause in determining the habit of onanism is a redundant prepuce. Around the corona glandis, in the sulcus, are situated a number of sebaceous glands, the secretion of which, if allowed to accumulate, excites irritation and itching. Erection and the venereal orgasm follow the friction which is innocently used to allay the itching. Moreover, when the glans is habitually covered, it becomes morbidly excita-

* London Hospital Reports, vol. ii. p. 58.

ble, and the least friction develops the special sensibility of its nerves.

According to Simon* (*de Metz*) various causes besides the foregoing increase the excitement of the genitals at puberty, among which he enumerates prolonged sitting, as at school, which fatigues the spinal column and causes an accumulation of blood in the inferior parts of the trunk. "For the same reason," says Simon, "that clerks and persons who ride much on horseback or in carriages are exposed to hemorrhoids, boys will experience excitement of the genitals in consequence of engorgement of the testes and spermatic cord."

Patients frequently refer the origin of the habit of masturbation to the influence and example of older boys. In public institutions, where many boys of the more depraved sort are collected together, this may sometimes occur; and even in the better class of boarding-schools a bad boy, given to this vice, may induce others to commence it; but generally speaking, the remark of Quintilian is true: *Non accipiunt e scholis mala ista, sed in scholas afferunt.* The masturbator takes

* *Traité d'Hygiène appliquée à l'Education de la Jeunesse.* Paris, 1827, p. 164.

into the school those organic tendencies which lead to the perpetration of the vice. Possessing the erotic temperament, slight causes will suffice, at school or at home, to awaken the special sensibility of the sexual apparatus.

Under what circumstances soever the vice of masturbation may be contracted, it is usually continued, and with increasing frequency, until weakness of the genital organs and various functional derangements are produced. The habit is discontinued, either because of some evident ill consequence which alarms the patient, or he is informed of the serious results which must finally ensue from his violation of a natural law. But the unfortunate victim finds that the cessation or diminution of the habit does not restore him to the natural state. He cannot rid his imagination of the erotic fancies which have so long possessed it. During sleep lascivious dreams beset him, accompanied by the venereal orgasm and the seminal loss. During the day erotic ideas constantly invade his mind, and partial erections occur, followed by a tenacious discharge which slowly escapes from the urethra.

It is probable, also, that spermatorrhœa may

result from excesses in natural coitus. Cases apparently originating in this way have fallen under my observation. The history of these cases is as follows: After very free indulgence symptoms have occurred indicating the necessity for abstinence. This sudden and forced continence puts the mind of the individual and his genital apparatus in the same condition as that which occurs after the habit of masturbation ceases.

The relation which spermatorrhœa bears to certain structural alterations of the genito-urinary organs requires to be carefully investigated. Very contradictory opinions have been expressed on this point.

By surgeons it is regarded as an affection—an inflammation or an irritation—of a part of the genito-urinary apparatus, and the surgical treatment is based upon this pathological doctrine. One of the most recent and able of surgical authorities* treats of it under the heading of "functional disorders of the testicle." The modern surgical writers in general adopt this view, especially those accessible to the American

* Holmes's System of Surgery—Art., Diseases of the Male Organs. Vol. iv., p. 539. London. 1864.

reader.* The work of Lallemand† is the principal source of these pathological views. It will be proper, therefore, to present an outline of this author's doctrines before presenting our own.

Views of M. Lallemand.—This author regards the following as playing an important *rôle* in the production of this disorder: Blenorrhagia and stricture of the urethra, the former affecting the prostatic part of the urethra and the orifices of the seminal ducts, and the latter producing dilatation of the ducts by the efforts of micturition; gouty and rheumatic affections occurring in these parts; accumulation of sebaceous matter under the prepuce, constituting a source of irritation; venereal excesses and masturbation, which act principally by provoking inflammation or irritation of the ducts; prolonged erections excited

* Gross's System of Surgery, p. 831–2, vol. ii. Phila.: 1865. Erichsen's Surgery, p. 1224. A Practical Treatise on the Disease of the Testis, etc., by Curling. Phila. Ed., p. 326, *et. seq.*, etc., etc., etc.

† *Des Pertes Séminales Involontaires*, op. cit. Also, *Observations sur les Maladies des Organes Genito-Urinaires. Première Partie*, p. 158 *et seq.*, 1825, by the same author. The influence of a "hobby" is well seen in the growth of M. Lallemand's opinions and practices during the fifteen years' interval between these works.

by erotic ideas or lascivious publications; the use of diuretics, of ergot, of cantharides, etc.; the abuse of alcoholic drinks, of coffee, and of tea; constipation; ascarides in the rectum; hemorrhoids; fissures of the anus; heating and irritation of the anal and perineal regions by habitual sitting, or prolonged horseback riding.

The organic peculiarities which predispose to spermatorrhœa are, according to this author—excessive length of the prepuce; hypospadias; extraordinary size of the meatus urethræ; flaccidity of the corpora cavernosa; smallness, tardy descent and lack of firmness of the testes; relaxation of the cord and of the scrotum; varicocele; congenital induration of the prostate, and great development of the pelvis with feminine characters.

When the nocturnal pollutions are due to excesses, to abuse, to the presence of ascarides in the rectum, they produce, according to Lallemand, grave disorders in a short time after their appearance. After a little, all the phenomena of excitation which precede or accompany the orgasm diminish, and finally completely disappear; the act of emission occurring without erection, pleasure, or any particular sensation. The semen loses little by little its color, its odor, and its spermatozoa, and comes to resemble, more and more, either mucus or the prostatic fluid. This progressive diminution in the excitation of the genital organs, and this increasing alteration in the sperm, corrèspond with a remarkable augmentation in the gravity of the general symptoms and in the difficulties in the treatment. At the same time the vesiculæ seminales acquire the power of contracting under the influence of a less energetic excitement. Then, also, fulness of the bladder or rectum, a warm, soft bed, lying on the back, warm drinks, excitants, etc., provoke emissions more or less easily. The effects are much more serious when to the nocturnal are added diurnal pollutions. Some patients suffer only fróm nocturnal pollutions, but such cases are rare.

The diurnal pollutions, according to Lallemand, are produced by all those causes which increase constipation and favor the excitation of the genital organs; such as prolonged sitting, the jolting of a carriage, riding on horseback, etc. In some subjects the pollution does not take place passively during the efforts of defecation, and by the simple effects of compression, but by the proper action of the ejaculatory apparatus. These cases are unusual. In all the others the semen is emitted without the sensible phenomena of ejaculation. The evil effects are determined by the abundance of the loss; but some persons support the losses better than others.

The varieties of noctural and diurnal pollutions manifest themselves successively or simultaneously. The specific character is the sudden expulsion of semen in notable quantities at variable intervals. A symptom which has close relation to spermatorrhœa, and which ordinarily accompanies it, is impotence. In all cases of nocturnal or diurnal pollutions, the first symptom discovered is a notable diminution in the energy and duration of the erections, and an increased readiness of ejaculation.

M. Lallemand gives the following result of his microscopic examinations of the excreted matters in the different varieties of seminal loss: "When the evacuations are rare and the semen has preserved its distinctive characters, the animalcules present nothing remarkable either in respect to numbers or dimensions. But when the spermatorrhœa has assumed sufficient importance to influence the rest of the economy, the semen becomes more liquid, and the animalcules are less developed and less vivacious, although their number may not appear to be diminished. When the erections commence to diminish, the semen is more aqueous; the dimensions of the spermatozoa are sometimes one-fourth or one-third their normal size, their caudal prolongation being distinguishable with difficulty, with a power of 300 diameters." *

The central idea of M. Lallemand's theory of the pathology of spermatorrhœa, is the production, by various causes, of an irritation or inflammation of the prostatic portion of the urethra and of the seminal ducts. This view is not supported by anatomical evidence. Although cadaveric examinations, as is well said by M. Raige-Delorme,† have resulted in the discovery of diverse alterations of the genital organs in cases in which seminal losses *were presumed* to have ex-

* Op. cit., II. p. 404.

† *Dictionnaire de Médecine*, vol. xxviii., p. 506.

isted, these alterations were so connected with important diseases of other parts of the genito-urinary apparatus, that little reliance can be placed in them as indicative of spermatorrhœa. These alterations consisted in ulcerations of the orifices of the ejaculatory ducts; injection and ulceration of various parts of these canals; analogous alterations of the vesiculæ seminales; purulent depots in the vesicles, in the vasa deferentia, in the epididymis, in the body of Highmore, and in the testicle. It is impossible to associate these lesions with spermatorrhœa, since in all the cases cited they were accompanied by more or less grave alterations of the urinary passages. One cannot avoid the reflection in looking over Lallemand's cases, published in his work on the genito-urinary organs in 1825, and in his work on seminal losses in 1839, that his cases as well as his theory were constructed to justify his practice. There is no proof that the anatomical lesions described by this author were causative of spermatorrhœa, or that they were even accompanied by it. On the other hand, the observations are numerous enough in which these alterations occurred without the production of spermatorrhœa. The truth is, undoubtedly, that there is no specific anatomical element in all that Lallemand has submitted, to be associated indissolubly with that disorder, and to which it may be attributed. In support of our opinion, we may cite the high authority of Mr. Thompson,* who asserts that inordinate sexual indulgence cannot have the effect to produce prostatitis unless gonorrhœa be already existing.

I may also refer, in opposition to the views of Lallemand, to my personal observations. As pathologist to the Cincinnati Hospital, and during the time of my military experiences, I have had numerous opportunities to ascertain—if it exist—a causative relation between the lesions of the generative apparatus and spermatorrhœa described by Lallemand, but hitherto have failed to observe this connection. To place this question beyond controversy I have lately made a most careful dissection of the sexual apparatus of a young man dead of a double pneumonia, who was known to have practised masturbation in an extreme degree for many years. Besides a catarrhal

* On Enlarged Prostate: Its Pathology and Treatment. London, 1858, p. 195.

condition of the mucous membrane of the seminal and prostatic ducts, and of the *vesiculæ seminales*, there was literally no lesion of these organs. I therefore reject this position of Lallemand as untenable, and as leading to improper methods of treatment.

The views of Lallemand in regard to the alterations in the spermatozoids, and their destruction in advanced cases of spermatorrhœa, are hardly more tenable than his doctrine of the structural alterations peculiar to this disease. Liégeois, who has examined this question, remarks: "My own observations (six cases) are not at all in accordance with the description given by Lallemand. Azoospermia, existed in only one of my patients. The other five, though the involuntary emissions were frequent, and the virile faculties had materially diminished, though the affection had lasted from two to ten years, I have never found any change in the aspect, the consistency, or the odor of the seminal fluid, not even in the number or the configuration of the spermatoza.*" This accords with my own observation.

* The Seminal Secretion in Disease. *Medical Times and Gazette*, Nov. 6, 1869.

Spermatorrhœa is, in the view of the author, a *neurosis.* Although structural alterations may be coincident, they are not causative. It is certainly true, however, that lesions of various parts of the generative organs may increase that disorder of their nervous apparatus which finds expression in frequent involuntary seminal losses. In order to a just comprehension of spermatorrhœa, our inquiry must start from the physiology of the normal coitus. The seminal ejaculation is a reflex act. The sensation excited by friction of the erect and turgid male organ is transmitted to the cord, and the impression is reflected over the testes, vesiculæ seminales, urethra, and appended muscular apparatus, producing the seminal ejaculation. The whole constitutes the venereal orgasm.* It approximates in many of its phenomena to epilepsy, and is accompanied in some persons with an epileptiform seizure. This is more particularly exhibited

* Carpenter's Physiology, 5th ed. p. 794. Kirke's Physiology, p. 411. On this point the reader may consult with great advantage the elaborate work by Luys entitled *Recherches sur le Système Nerveux Cérébro-Spinal, sa Structure ses Fonctions et ses Maladies.* Paris, 1865, pp. 296 and 339.

in the act of masturbation, in which the excitation of the genital organs is more intense, the imagination more inflamed, and the orgasm more profound. There is a great expenditure of nervous force in a single act of coitus—much more so in the unlawful excitation—manifested by the languor, weakness, and mental feebleness which occur for some time afterwards. Of course, these effects will be experienced in a much greater degree when the orgasm is frequently repeated.

The generative apparatus of the male and female has a very intimate relation with the nervous system. It is the impression which the individuals of each sex make upon the organs of sense that excites those desires which have coitus for their object. There is a corresponding influence of the genital organs upon the nervous centres; for when semen accumulates in the reservoirs, the organs of generation transmit an influence to the cerebro-spinal centres, giving rise to sexual desire.

"The glans penis," says Kobelt,* "is the principal point of reunion of the sensitive nerves of

* *De l'appareil du sens génital.* Strasbourg: 1851; quoted by Luys.

the virile organ; no other part which it regulates can be compared with it in this respect. In respect to richness in nerves, the glans penis yields to no other part of the economy, not even the organs of sense." According to Kobelt,* the division of the dorsal nerve of the penis, in the most powerful and erotic stallion, deprives the animal of sexual desire as completely as castration.

"Anatomically regarded," says Handfield Jones, "it is very remarkable how closely the different nervous centres, or parts of a nervous centre, are connected by commissural fibres; and from a pathological point of view, the same connection is very manifest. The general exhaustion induced by excess in venery; the production of neuralgia in weakly persons by bodily exercise; the effect of muscular exertion in causing drowsiness—are examples which show how excessive consumption of nerve-force in one part weakens it also in others," etc.

Experience has abundantly shown that the lesions resulting from masturbation are those due to expenditure of nervous force and derange-

* *De l'appareil du sens génital.* Op. cit., as quoted by Luys.

ment of the intimate and harmonious relation existing between the sexual system and cerebro-spinal centres, and not to a mere loss of seminal fluid; for under no other circumstances is so small a discharge from the body accompanied by such serious results. This conclusion is further strengthened by the more important effects which follow masturbation than spermatorrhœa, although the mere seminal loss in two cases may be exactly equal.

A marked feebleness of the intellectual faculties is observed after abuse; other parts of the nervous system also participate in the debility of the encephalon. The organs of sense, especially that of vision, lose their sensibility to their appropriate stimuli, and their functional activity is lowered.

By masturbation, by excesses in venery, a condition of hyperæsthesia of the glans and urethra is induced, and the reflex act of ejaculation becomes abnormally excitable. Under these circumstances erotic ideas are readily experienced, and so promptly does the reflex function of the cord respond, that the seminal loss may occur without a decided venereal orgasm.

This is the essential pathological condition in spermatorrhœa. By frequent involuntary losses a habit is induced, and power diminishes. This idea has been well expressed by Handfield Jones:—

"It seems a well-established fact that the nervous tissue, both in the centres and in the peripheral extensions, becomes more excitable and mobile in proportion as its power becomes weaker. The motor nerve is more readily thrown into action, though the impulse it communicates is weak, and cannot be long sustained." *

The physiological origin of spermatorrhœa must not be overlooked. As I have already indicated, adults in full health have emissions, when continent, more or less frequently, according to their sexual peculiarities. This spontaneous evacuation is an effort of nature, under these circumstances, to supply the lack of use of a physiological function. That such occasional loss is physiological rather than pathological, seems confirmed by the good effects which ensue from it upon the mental and physical constitution of the individual. The inquietude of

* Functional Nervous Diseases, op. cit., p. 48.

mind, the headache, and the hebetude of body which are experienced anterior to the evacuation become relieved thereby; the muscular movements are then more easily executed; the headache ceases, and the mental operations are more rapid and clear. In some subjects, however, these evacuations may become so frequent and excessive as to constitute a pathological state. This occurs in clergymen, in studious persons of sedentary habits, and in those whose nervous apparatus has been deranged by dyspepsia. The excessive use of such stimulants as coffee and tobacco by continent persons who have weak digestion, slight muscular development, and a preponderating nervous system, powerfully contributes to the conversion of a physiological into a pathological spermatorrhœa.

Moral.—Foremost amongst the moral causes must be placed the indulgence in lascivious thoughts, which acts by maintaining a state of turgescence of the sexual apparatus.

During this condition of excitement semen is abundantly secreted, and accumulating in the *vesiculæ seminales*, must find an outlet by the nocturnal loss. Frequent repetition of this excitement induces that condition of irritability of the sexual organs, the essential cause of spermatorrhœa. Similar to this in all respects is the effect of that venereal excitement caused by taking liberties with the opposite sex without the gratification of desire. The intimate relation which exists between parties "engaged to be married," if long continued, frequently produces the same condition of genital weakness.

SYMPTOMS.

The signs and symptoms of spermatorrhœa may be divided into the *objective* and *subjective;* the objective being those which are recognised by the physician; the subjective those of which the patient himself only is conscious. It is not always possible to separate the symptoms due to masturbation from those of spermatorrhœa. There is a practical utility in placing them side by side for the purpose of comparison. The two conditions are so frequently united, and the connection between them of cause and effect so intimate, that the symptoms of both may be comprehended in the experience of the same individual. It is to be remarked that the voluntary seminal losses by unnatural means are much more active in producing the various secondary phenomena of this disorder, than the involuntary. The former are manifested, also, by more positive objective signs.

Objective Symptoms due to Masturbation.—Objectively considered, the masturbator is recognised by a marked facial expression, by a characteristic mannerism, and by a peculiar mental state.

The facial expression consists of a pale and sallow tint of the skin; unusual development of acne, especially on the forehead; a dark circle around the orbits; dilated and sluggish pupils; lustreless eyes, and an oblique line extending from the inner angle of the lids transversely across the cheek to the lower margin of the malar bone. The face has a haggard, troubled, furtive expression. These signs of themselves are by no means conclusive, for they may be produced by other causes than masturbation. This observation is especially true with respect to acne. This eruption occurs at puberty, more or less abundantly in different temperaments; and hence it would be very unjust to accuse young men of practising onanism in whom no other evidence of the fact existed than the presence of this eruption.

The manner of the masturbator is peculiar. He is listless, shy, retiring, and easily confused; he avoids society, preferring solitude; there is a want of steadiness and decision in his locomotion; his inferior extremities seem deficient in power, and all his movements betray a mind ill at ease.

His mental operations are confused; his speech is embarrassed, awkward, and without directness; his memory is defective, and he is absent-minded and given to reverie. If the habit has long existed, and been excessively frequent in repetition, epilepsy may be produced; or serious mental disorder, as delusional insanity, dementia, etc., may occur.

The state of the genital organs varies with the length of time the habit has been indulged. In some young subjects, there will be observed an extraordinary development of the organs, owing to premature excitement; but the disproportion is not maintained. With the progress of the habit the penis becomes relaxed, the erections feeble; the corpora cavernosa either atrophy or their vessels lose their tonicity, whereby an apparent diminution in bulk takes place; the corpus spongiosum and the glans also shrink, so that the prepuce appears unnaturally elongated. The testes may increase in size, become tender and "irritable," or they may undergo a certain degree of atrophy; the latter is the more usual result. In addition to these signs, a strong and sometimes overpowering spermatic odor is observed about these parts, and may diffuse itself in the atmosphere around the patient.

SUBJECTIVE SYMPTOMS DUE TO MASTURBATION.— Pains in the lumbar region, a sense of weight and aching in the loins, around the anus, and in the testes, are experienced. The appetite is capricious, the digestion feeble, and the bowels are constipated, or constipation alternates with diarrhœa.

The mind is deficient in power of attention; the imagination is constantly pervaded with vague erotic dreams, the moral sense is blunted, and the perceptions are dull and confused. Pains in the head, in the occipital and frontal regions, and a sense of fulness, and in serious cases alarming vertigo; pains in the course of the principal nerves, and an extreme nervous susceptibility are experienced. The organic nervous system manifests a functional disturbance in harmony with the disorder of the nervous system of animal life. Gastralgia and abdominal pain and uneasiness are in some cases very distressing symptoms.

The distinctiveness of the foregoing symptoms will be determined by the extent and duration of the habit, and by the constitutional peculiarities of the patient. The more highly developed the nervous system, and the more it preponderates in activity over the muscular and digestive systems, the more serious the effects.

Objective Symptoms of Spermatorrhœa.—These are in many respects similar to those due to masturbation. The same cause, indeed, is in operation, but is much less powerful.

The facial expression is not so marked. Acne is not common. The discoloration of the eye-lids is decided only in cases of very frequent seminal loss. The face is usually pale, sallow, and thin, anxious or sad in advanced cases. The manner is more or less retiring, subdued, and melancholy. Effeminacy, and sometimes extreme pusillanimity, are observed. Society is distasteful, or is absolutely avoided. Memory and power of attention are defective, and the patient is subject to fits of depression and melancholy, and is absorbed in the contemplation of his infirmity. These mental effects are frequently greatly disproportioned to the real importance of the malady; they are increased by popular works on this subject, for the perusal of which these patients have a prodigious *penchant*. They imagine themselves possessed of every infirmity portrayed in these works, and are not unfrequently driven to the verge of insanity by their apprehensions. Hypochondria is a very constant mental symptom; but true mental alienation is not, by any means, so frequently observed as in masturbation.

The genital organs are relaxed, the scrotum pendent, the veins of the spermatic cord varicose, the erections deficient in power and duration, and the seminal fluid is thin, watery; the spermatozoa are deficient in size and activity, and are imperfect in development. The urine is pale, of low specific gravity, and loaded with urates. An evident feebleness of the general system exists, manifested by a quick, weak pulse, cold hands and feet, hurried respiration, and loss of flesh and muscular vigor.

SUBJECTIVE SYMPTOMS OF SPERMATORRHŒA.— Weakness in the back and pain extending upwards to the scapula; pain along the spermatic cord, in the hips, around the anus, and pain in micturition, are experienced by the patient. He has a variable appetite, and suffers from dyspepsia, borborygmi, constipation, and diarrhœa. He complains of weakness in the knees, with pain and soreness of the calves, and loss of power in the inferior extremities. His sensations in these parts may be perverted. He has also headache, or a sense of fulness in the head; he can fix his mind on any subject with difficulty; his attention wanders, and he is given to day-dreams and to erotic visions.

The importance of the foregoing symptoms will be governed by the frequency of the spermal losses. They are felt in the greatest intensity on the morning succeeding the nocturnal emissions.

The essential symptom in spermatorrhœa is the occurrence of seminal losses. Lallemand, and succeeding writers following him, divide these into *nocturnal* and *diurnal* pollutions. The nocturnal occur at night in an erotic dream, with a more or less decided venereal orgasm; and their importance, in a pathological point of view, will be wholly determined by the frequency of their occurrence, and the evident derangements of the organism which precede or accompany them.

The diurnal pollutions, according to Lallemand, occur principally in micturition and defecation; passively in some subjects, owing to a superabundance of semen in the vesiculæ seminales; in others with a certain pleasure and a definite ejaculation; and in others, habitually, without sensation, with a feeble or scarcely perceptible ejaculatory effort. The first variety can hardly be regarded as pathological.

It is peculiarly unfortunate that these views of M. Lallemand, with reference to diurnal pollutions, have obtained such general credence. The minds of patients become so impressed with the conviction that every mucous flow from the urethra is seminal, that it is difficult to overcome it. They parade this symptom and dwell upon it, believing that it has the pathological significance which Lallemand and his followers have ascribed to it.

The various symptoms of spermatorrhœa may be comprehended in three groups: genital; cerebral; spinal.

In the first, or genital form or phase, which is the most common, there are excessive sensibility of the sexual apparatus, and greatly increased reflex excitability of the cord.

In the cerebral form there are associated with the preceding condition certain disorders of the mind—melancholia, delusional insanity, and mania.

In the spinal form the functional derangement of the cord is either excessive and pronounced, or has resulted in organic lesion.

I.—GENITAL FORM.

The sexual organs are relaxed; the testes tender, painful, and sometimes wasted; the erections feeble and the seminal flow watery. Slight causes—an erotic idea, gentle friction, a voluptuous dream—will produce a feeble erection followed by a quick emission with but little sensation. Whenever an erection and an emission occur, there is an evident orgasm, but not nearly so pronounced as in the normal state. After every erection without seminal loss, there is a mucous flow from the urethra. A mixture of this mucus with the semen produces the so-called watery semen. The same mucous discharge is not unfrequently observed after urination and defecation. It alarms the patient, because he has been led to believe that it is seminal. These are the cases to which M. Lallemand applies the term "diurnal pollution." If a proper examination of this fluid be made, it will be found not to contain spermatozoa. It is a thick, transparent, albuminous fluid, alkaline in reaction, and presents under the microscope the cellular elements noted in Fig. 1. We need hardly remark that the presence of spermatozoa (Fig. 2.) is essential to prove the existence of semen. No other test is at all applicable to the determination of this question, than the microscopic. It cannot be denied that spermatozoa may be found in the urine or mucous secretion from the urethra, if a nocturnal emission, or an emission produced by natural or unnatural means, have recently occurred; but these fluids should be examined, when this source of error may be eliminated. We are glad to have an opportunity of quoting in support of our opinion so able an observer as Prof. Flint,* who

* Practice of Medicine: H. C. Lea. Phila., 1866.

remarks on this subject—"In the most of these cases the fluid is either the *liquor prostaticus* or a secretion from the vesiculæ seminales. The microscope affords the only mode of determining that the fluid is seminal. Were this mode of examination generally adopted, cases of spermatorrhœa would be extremely rare." We quote further some excellent remarks on this subject from Hassell:* "Care must be taken not to confound the discharge of urethral gleet with the seminal fluid; the distinction is easy, since the former is distinguished by the absence of infusoria, by the presence of scaly epithelium, and by the escape being in general continuous. Sometimes the gleety discharge occurs only after sexual excitement and lasts but for a short time, when, of course, its character is more apt to be mistaken. The prostatic fluid might also be mistaken for semen; in this the spermatozoa would also be absent, and in addition, the microscope would reveal in it the presence of the prostatic cylinders, and perhaps, also, of the peculiar lamellated concretions of phosphate of lime, which

* The Urine in Health and Disease. London: 1863.

are found in the prostate in such numbers. Like the mucus from ordinary gleet, that from the prostate may also be continuous, but more frequently it appears only after violent efforts at defecation, when a small quantity of matter may be expressed, forming only a drop or two, of a thick, stringy, and transparent fluid, which appears at the orifice of the urethra." Dr. Chambers,* in a lecture delivered at St. Mary's Hospital, expressed his conviction that this mucous flow from the urethra has no more pathological significance than the leucorrhœa of woman. He further asserts that true spermatorrhœa is a rare, almost unknown disease, but he evidently here refers to that constant stillicidium of semen to which Lallemand gave the name diurnal pollutions, and which many writers consider, but erroneously, the true spermatorrhœa. Again, Dunglison† says, "the presence of such a fluid in these circumstances, by no means shows that it is sperm.

* Lecture on Gonorrhœa and Imaginary Spermatorrhœa. delivered at St. Mary's Hospital, June 14, 1861. Lancet, 1861.

† Cyclopædia of Practical Medicine. Am. Ed., Vol. II. p. 212.

Indeed, it probably rarely is so, and is nothing more than the mucous fluid from the prostate or Cowper's glands." It seems a labor of supererogation to multiply authorities on this point. There can be no question that this mucous fluid is derived from the prostate, vesiculæ seminales, Cowper's glands, and from the follicles of the urethra. The frequent excitement accompanied by increased blood supply, to which these parts are subjected, must induce a greater secretory activity in their glandular appendages. Hence we should expect to find blennorrhagia in cases of masturbation or spermatorrhœa. The urethra is red, injected, and exceedingly sensitive, and considerable irritation is referred to the region of the neck of the bladder and prostate gland. No other anatomical lesions can, with propriety, be attributed to spermatorrhœa. If any other be present, they are merely accidental or accessory and not essential. In this category may be placed those lesions described by Lallemand: thickening and stricture of the urethra, ulceration of the seminal ducts, suppuration in the prostate, etc.

The phenomena of the genital form will be better exhibited by an illustrative case.

CASE I.—This was a patient, aged 32, who had practised masturbation with great frequency as a youth, but on learning the evil consequences had resolutely abandoned the habit. He afterwards suffered from frequent nocturnal emissions, and had, finally, such sensitiveness of the genital organs, that the slightest excitement produced a feeble erection and ejaculation. After micturition and defecation he had a thick, tenacious discharge, which gave him great concern. He had, also, considerable irritation of the bladder, pain and aching about the anus, in the back and loins. He was pale and thin; his appetite was capricious, and he suffered much from constipation, pain in the abdomen, borborygmi, and flatulence. His pulse was quick; hands and feet cool and damp. His special senses were unimpaired; he had no mental aberration in any form; he was despondent and brooded over his sexual condition, fearing impotence. Although more easily fatigued than usual, he was still capable of very considerable exertion. His sexual desire was not materially lessened, for he had contracted a marriage engagement with which he feared to comply. His fears had been aroused by advertisements in the newspapers and popular works on his malady, for the reading of which he had the usual propensity. His organs were not materially damaged. The prepuce was long and the penis lax; the left testis was somewhat atrophied, owing, probably, to a varicose condition of the veins of the cord on that side.

The cases of the genital form of spermatorrhœa vary very much in importance. They occupy all possible intermediate gradations between the pale and emaciated subject who suffers from nightly pollutions and severe gastric and cardiac symptoms, and the plethoric subject whose weekly nocturnal loss is an expression of a necessity of his sexual nature.

II.—CEREBRAL FORM.

The most serious mental effects are produced by masturbation. This vice, commenced at the period of puberty, interferes seriously with the development of the brain and the evolution of the mental faculties. We have already seen that this sad habit is contracted by those in whom the nervous apparatus predominates in activity over the muscular and digestive, and in whom the imaginative faculties are more highly cultivated than the reason and judgment. The mental effects of spermatorrhœa are also marked in those cases which we have denominated the cerebral.

It is to be remarked that the mental phenomena of spermatorrhœa are not always in proportion to the seminal losses. In the cerebral form, in addition to those lesions of the sexual spinal system, of the digestive apparatus, and of the circulation, described under the genital form, there are certain disorders of the mind. That spermatorrhœa will produce in one class of cases mental disorders, and not in another, indicates either that some predisposition to these disorders existed, or that the habit of self-pollution was merely an expression of mental alienation. The lascivious images which pervade the minds of boys possessed of the highly developed nervous organization of masturbators are those of delusional insanity. In one case the spermatorrhœa is a symptom of mental disorder; in the other, the spermatorrhœa is an exciting cause—the predisposition already existing.

There is, however, a cerebral phase of spermatorrhœa which may be separated from the two preceding classes. It is characterized by indistinctness of vision, dilatation of the pupil, amblyopia, diplopia; diminution in the sensitiveness of the auditory apparatus; feebleness of voice; mental preoccupation, hebetude of mind, confusion of ideas, and a profound melancholy. "Patients who have been laboring under spermatorrhœa for a series of years are much more liable to hypochondriasis and cerebral affection than to tabes dorsalis," says Romberg.* Not only do long-continued and excessive seminal losses produce these cerebral symptoms, but they may occur in those unhappy individuals who have acquired very false and highly-colored views of their condition from popular works on the subject. The termination of such cases is in suicidal monomania, delusional insanity, etc.

In that variety of the cerebral form in which a decided predisposition must be admitted to exist, to disorder of the intellectual faculties, there are found various forms of mental alienation. The chronic form is the most common, which cor-

* Vol. II., p. 400.

responds to the *melancholia* of Pinel, or the *lypemania* of Esquirol, terminating in *dementia*. Several of the most characteristic cases which have happened under my observation correspond to the *delusional insanity* of Bucknill and Tuke.* Many writers are disposed to underrate the importance of this tendency in spermatorrhœa. To the influence of quack advertisements and popular works, which, of course, greatly exaggerate the evils of this disease, is ascribed the melancholy, the hypochondriasis, and other mental disorders which occur in the course of it. The statistics of any of our large insane asylums will illustrate the influence of masturbation in the production of mental alienation. We have already given the opinion of Romberg on this point. Mr. Holmes Coote, in a discussion which followed Dr. Drysdale's paper on the "Medical Aspects of Prostitution," read before the Harveian Society of London, remarked that "he still entertained the opinion that there were worse evils appertaining to human weakness than prostitution. He had opportunities of witnessing the fact that among the young there was no cause

* Manual of Psychological Medicine. Phila. Ed., p. 103.

of insanity more common than indulging in habits which he would not further particularize, but which were known to result in the most complete bodily and mental prostration."* Dr. John P. Gray, the distinguished Superintendent of the State Asylum at Utica, New York, thus speaks† of the influence of masturbation in the production of insanity:—"The records of this institution show five hundred and twenty-one cases admitted directly attributable to this vice, and I am well convinced that the number is greatly understated." We might add confirmatory testimony from a variety of sources, but the foregoing is sufficient for our purpose.

The cerebral form is exhibited in the following typical cases:

Case ii.—Was a young man admitted to St. John's Hospital as a private patient; æt. 30; five feet five inches high; leuco-phlegmatic temperament; beard scanty; hair thin. At the time of admission he could not give a rational account

* British Medical Journal, Feb. 17, 1866.

† Twenty-fourth Annual Report. 1867.

of himself. His eye was wild; pupil very much dilated; face pale, thin, and haggard. He walked unsteadily because of disturbance of cerebral circulation; he was "dizzy." At night he was given up to various hallucinations; he did not sleep, but spent the night in talking in a wild and incoherent manner, in wandering about his room, and beating upon the walls. During the day he was quiet, but his conversation was disconnected, his ideas wandering, and his speech confused. His appetite was capricious, his bowels constipated, and he had suffered greatly from borborygmi and abdominal pain. From his brother it was ascertained that he had been greatly addicted to natural and unnatural venereal excitement, and had suffered lately from frequent involuntary losses. The state of his genital organs confirmed this.

Case iii.—Was similar to the preceding—a young man who had passed several years in the military service, during which time he had indulged very freely in the vice of masturbation. He was led to St. John's Hospital by a comrade; he could not walk without support, in consequence, he said, of "lightness of his head." He had neither delirium nor hallucinations, but he was reduced to a state of mental feebleness bordering on dementia. He was pale, thin, and had little appetite; his vision was indistinct; his pupils were dilated, and his hearing was dull and indistinct. All of his senses, indeed, were in a state of torpor. He admitted a degree of self-abuse, extending over several years, too revolting to be narrated, and had lately, after discontinuing it, suffered from a pitiable degree of seminal weakness.*

III.—SPINAL FORM.

Impairment of locomotion and spinal paralysis have long been associated with venereal excesses. The progressive spinal paralysis, the tabes dorsalis of the Germans, and the *ataxie locomotrice progressive* of Duchenne, was formerly confounded with the effects of masturbation and excesses in venery. The differential diagnosis will be a subject for future consideration.

* Both of these cases formed the subject of a Clinical Lecture at St. John's Hospital, before the class of the Medical College of Ohio. Session of 1865–1866.

In the spinal form of spermatorrhœa there are weakness of inferior extremities, altered—diminished or perverted—and referred sensations, incontinence of urine and fæces, and sometimes paraplegia. These symptoms are additional to those described as pertaining to the genital form; they may also be superadded to the cerebral. In the following typical case, it will be seen that the spinal symptoms were distinctive.

Case iv.—A travelling showman, æt. 35, came under my care, suffering from weakness, with perverted sensations of both inferior extremities. He had an ill-conditioned ulcer on the right leg; slight pressure, as of riding on horseback, induced intractable ulcerations of buttocks and thighs. He had also, to a limited extent, incontinence both of urine and fæces. The sensibility of the skin, as to touch, pain, pressure, and the electric current, was diminished. He had a sense of formication in his legs and tingling in his feet. The tendo-achillis of each side was a little shortened. He volunteered the information that earlier in life he had been much addicted to onanism, and that since the habit was discontinued he had suffered from frequent nocturnal emissions. His mental powers were unimpaired. He had the unavoidable depression and anxiety arising from his very miserable physical condition, and nothing more.

In what does the spinal lesion consist in these cases? We have stated that the important pathological condition in the genital form of spermatorrhœa is a morbid excitability of the reflex faculty, with congestion, probably of the cord. In the spinal form there is probably some structural lesion inappreciable by our ordinary means of investigation, a molecular change, possibly, or the nervous phenomena are of the reflex character. We have, however, no anatomical facts on which to base the former opinion—our knowledge of these cases being entirely clinical; but the symptoms and the results of treatment seem to confirm our view of the pathology. Schroeder van der Kolk,* also, has made some observations which tend to establish the same view. Says this able observer: "Onanism is commonly considered, and often correctly, to be a cause of epilepsy; but onanism and excitement of the sexual

* On the Minute Structure and Functions of the Spinal Cord and Medulla Oblongata. Syd. Soc. Translation, p. 268.

organs are, to a greater degree than is usually supposed, the result of irritation and congestion of the medulla oblongata. The opinion formerly advanced by Gall as to the localization of the sexual impulse in the cerebellum, has been sufficiently refuted, and the close relation between the medulla oblongata and the action of the genital organs, is generally received by physiologists. Let it suffice to call to mind the occurrence of erection and emission in persons hanged, how the sexual action is exalted in idiopathic mania with irritation of the brain and medulla oblongata; how frequently, after injuries of the part, erection and emission, or perhaps impotence is observed. * * * * In the case of epilepsy I have just recorded this influence was very evident; the emissions disappeared for a time, when the sensibility and over irritation of the medulla oblongata had again discharged themselves in a fit. * * It is but a short time since a similar case occurred to me, of a young man who was unable to continue his studies regularly on account of epilepsy, apparently originating in onanism. A few days ago I received a report, that for the last three months, after an issue had been by my advice established in the neck, neither the involuntary pollutions, which in this case also were very frequent, nor the epileptic attacks, which commonly returned every two or three weeks, had again appeared, while the patient's head had become much clearer, and he was able to continue his studies."

On the other hand Gull relates* a case of complete paraplegia, produced by sexual excess, in which no structural alteration of the cord could be detected, even by the most careful microscopic examination. This case is justly regarded as exceptional.

* Guy's Hospital Reports, 1858, p. 174.

RESULTS.

I have already sufficiently shown that various forms of mental derangement may accompany frequent involuntary losses. I need not waste space by recapitulating the observations on this topic.

An ordinary result of spermatorrhœa is weakness of mind. The brain acts slowly and imperfectly because a large part of the produced nerve-force is consumed in the frequently repeated venereal orgasm. These patients are dull and listless. To accomplish a given amount of intellectual labor, they find that an unusual effort is necessary. They are given to reverie, and to vague and shadowy dreams in which erotic phantasms play. They take little interest in business and in the affairs of life, and to this cause is to be attributed, in many instances, unexpected failure in business and professional pursuits. They are men of dreams instead of men of ideas and action. This condition of the mental and moral forces is a more frequent result of spermatorrhœa than mental derangement, properly speaking.

I have not observed any disorder of the special senses beyond the diminished sensibility due to increased consumption of nerve force in the sexual system.

The respiration becomes more or less irregular. Frequent deep inspirations, sighing, and a dry cough are often observed. Dryness of the fauces, especially of the posterior wall of the pharynx, and huskiness of voice also occur. I cannot say that I have observed phthisis to be produced by spermatorrhœa, neither do I believe that such result is probable; but, on the other hand, it is certainly true that if a tendency exist, hereditary or acquired, to this disease, frequent involuntary losses may promote its development, as indeed any cause may, which lowers the vital forces.

Irregular action of the heart is most common. Pains are felt in the præcordial region, the rhythm of the heart's movement is altered, and a subjective sense of fluttering is felt. These phenomena are frequently accompanied by a sense of constriction of the throat—a globus hystericus—a tendency to shed tears, and the emission of a plentiful quantity of pale urine.

The most serious results of spermatorrhœa are those produced in the generative organs themselves. Amongst these are impotence, "irritable testis," varicocele, and a state of hyperæsthesia of the spermatic plexus. Impotence should not be confounded with loss of procreating power. A man is said to be impotent when he is unable to perform the act of coitus. Capacity for sexual intercourse may exist without the power of procreation. The practice of masturbation, or spermatorrhœa, more usually results in impotence than in a mere loss of procreating power.

Long-continued excitation of the generative organs, whether by natural or unnatural means, so inflames the imagination and exalts the reflex faculty that emission occurs before intromission of the male organ can take place, or after very imperfect coitus. The latter is the more usual condition for which the physician is consulted. Patients are peculiarly fearful and sensitive on this point. The morbid apprehension under which they labor, greatly increases their incompetence. In some instances, without being at all seriously damaged in their sexual function, they are rendered temporarily impotent by the mere dread of failure. The London quack, Dr. Graham, understood the influence of the imagination upon the sexual congress. "Amongst the furniture of the 'Temple of Health' was a celestial bed, provided with costly draperies, and standing on glass legs. Married couples who slept on this couch were sure of being blessed with a beautiful progeny. For its use, one hundred pounds per night were demanded, and numerous persons of rank were foolish enough to comply with the terms." *

The impotence of spermatorrhœa is not a permanent condition, unless serious cerebral or spinal complications have occurred. Ordinarily, the capacity for coitus returns with the cessation of the seminal losses—the evidence of a healthy functional state of the spinal cord. The loss of procreating power is not a frequent accompaniment of seminal weakness; the difficulty is in the intromission of the organ. Every practical physician is cognizant of instances of men whose

* A Book about Doctors. Jeaffreson, p. 338.

semen had fertilizing power, but who were almost incapacitated for the sexual congress, by reason of a great excitability of the reflex faculty.

The same condition may exist as a result of long continence in ardent temperaments. But these cases only require a little time and familiarity with the object of desire.

Excluding from consideration those organic deficiencies which may produce impotence, as foreign to the purpose of this work, it will suffice to allude to varicocele, and so-called "irritable testes," when they are due to sexual abuses.

It is exceedingly doubtful whether varicocele confined to the left testis ever results in impotence. Some instances have occurred under my observation in which this disease produced atrophy of this testis, accompanied by a painful state of the right organ, and eventually resulting in almost complete extinction of sexual desire. In those exceptional and rare cases, where the varicocele is double, and atrophy results, impotence necessarily occurs.

To the increased activity of the testes in secreting semen, has been attributed the varicose condition of the spermatic veins in spermatorrhœa.

This view is hardly tenable. As the varicocele occurs on the left side almost invariably, in consequence of an anatomical peculiarity, and as it is not a constant nor even a frequent complication, we may consider its presence, in general, as accidental. Opposed to this view, we should not omit mention of Mr. Hutchison's * opinion, that varicocele is of spinal origin. Dr. Hughlings Jackson † has reported a case which seems to confirm this opinion of Mr. Hutchison.

The relation of "irritable testis" to impotence is much more immediate. By this term, Sir Astley Cooper,‡ to whom we are indebted for the most of our information on this subject, intended to express a state of hyperæsthesia of the spermatic plexus. One or both testes are painful, sometimes exquisitely so, tender to the touch, and occasionally swollen. The epididymis and spermatic cord also become so painful that the weight of the testes gives intolerable pain; and pain is experienced in the back and loins. Not-

* London Hospital Reports, vol. i., p. 77.

† Lancet, March 31, 1866.

‡ Observations on the Structure and Diseases of the Testis.—Chapter iv. London: 1830.

withstanding these symptoms, the testes are not hot and inflamed; the swelling is paroxysmal, and is not accompanied by fever. The general health is much impaired, partly in consequence of the suffering endured, and partly by reason of the disturbance of the nervous and digestive systems. The patient has a poor appetite; he suffers from indigestion; he is hysterical and despondent, and is unable to sleep. Impotence is a usual attendant on this state. Venereal excesses, masturbation, and spermatorrhœa, are the causes. At least we have frequently observed it to accompany spermatorrhœa, and in this case it proved the most troublesome and distressing symptom. The following case very well illustrates the signs and symptoms of this malady occurring in connection with seminal trouble.

Case v.—An Israelite, æt. 25, was admitted to St. John's Hospital, under the following circumstances: He had been married a week, but proved unable to consummate the sexual act, in consequence of which he was placed by his friends in a hospital to undergo treatment. He presented these symptoms: He was pale and sallow; his tongue coated; his appetite was poor; he had much abdominal pain, especially about the umbilicus, and he was constipated. The testes were very tender, constantly painful, especially when pendent, and the cord was also painful. The testes were subject to periodical attacks of enlargement, which lasted a few days and then subsided, there being, however, no redness nor increased heat, but only increased tenderness. He experienced various nervous symptoms; among others he had a well marked *globus hystericus*, and he shed tears on the least provocation. He admitted to very great sexual indulgences for several years, which were followed by spermatorrhœa. Since the occurrence of irritability of the testes, he had been entirely without sexual desire. He admitted that he had not been able to effect the sexual congress since his marriage.*

Even when it does not result in impotence, hyperæsthesia of the spermatic plexus produces

* This patient left the hospital after a stay of four weeks. He visited me recently, to assure me that he was restored to sexual soundness.

distressing nervous symptoms of a hysterical character. The various pelvic pains, occurring in spermatorrhœa, and referred to the prostate, neck of the bladder, rectum, perineum, and testes, are probably due to the same cause.

II.

SPERMATORRHŒA AS A SYMPTOM.

VARIOUS disorders of the nervous system, accompanied by frequent spermal losses, were, formerly, confounded with the results of seminal weakness. This was especially the case with the disease known as *tabes dorsalis*, which in the time of Hippocrates was assumed to be caused by venereal excesses. In the work *De Morbis* * occurs the following passage:

Tabes dorsalis a spinali medulla oritur, maxime vero recentes sponsos et libidinosos corripit. Febris sunt expertes, bene comedunt, et colliquantur. Quod si ita affectum perconteris, dicet, sibi videri ex superioribus partibus a capite velut formicas in spinam descendere; quumque urinam aut stercus reddit, ipse semen genitale copiosum et liquidum prodit; necque genitura intus con-

* Dr. Adams, the learned author of the Sydenham Society's edition of the works of Hippocrates, thinks the book *De Morbis* emanated from the Cnidian school.

cipitur et inter dormiendum cum uxore dormiat, nec ne semen profundat, etc. (Lib. ii., cap. 19.)

Celsus also alludes to similar effects produced by *nimia profusio seminis* which *tabe hominem consumat.**

Under the same designation similar effects have, since the time of Hippocrates, been ascribed to masturbation and venereal excesses by various German, French, and English writers. By Romberg,† however, the term "tabes dorsalis" is restricted to a nervous disease, identical with the progressive locomotor ataxia of Duchenne. On the other hand, so recent an authority as Dr. Meryon ‡ adheres to the ancient idea of tabes dorsalis, defining it as a "tractable form of paralysis, not unfrequently seen in youth and early manhood, which may be traced to the vicious and enervating habit of masturbation."

In progressive locomotor ataxia there occurs a peculiar degeneration of the posterior columns of

* De Medicina, lib. iv., p. 187. Edit. Milligan, Edinburgh: 1831.

† A Manual of the Nervous Diseases of Man. Edition of Syd. Society, translated by Sieveking, vol. ii., p. 395.

‡ Practical and Pathological Researches on the Various Forms of Paralysis, p. 44. London: 1864.

the cord : a gelatiniform degeneration of the nerve fibres and a hyperplasia of the intervening connective tissue. "Progressive abolition of co-ordination of movements and apparent paralysis, contrasting with integrity of the muscular force, are the fundamental characteristics," says Duchenne,* of this disease. According to this author, it is divisible as respects its symptomatology into three periods:

"1. Characterized by three symptoms—pains, ocular troubles, and anaphrodisia; 2d, by disorders of motility and of sensibility in the inferior extremities ; 3d, the extension of the same symptoms to the upper extremities." Before anaphrodisia, and the disorders of voluntary movement, symptoms referable to the generative organs are present. These symptoms are satyriasis and spermatorrhœa. In five cases of progressive locomotor ataxia, of which I have preserved full notes, more or less decided increase of the sexual appetite occurred in the inception of the disorder. Involuntary seminal losses are observed at the same time, and they attract the attention of the

* De l'Electrisation Localisée, etc. Deux. éd. Paris: 1861, p. 547.

patient more than any other symptom then present. It is in consequence of this fact that progressive locomotor ataxia was so long confounded with the results of excesses in venery. Trousseau* has especially called attention to these sexual symptoms which attend upon the first stage of this singular affection.

In some observations on this topic, Topinard † thus speaks of the symptoms in progressive locomotor ataxia, belonging to the generative organs:

"Four symptoms present themselves: spermatorrhœa, satyriasis, anaphrodisia, and impotence. The first occurs amongst the most remote antecedents of the first period, throughout which it continues. The nocturnal pollutions, at first accompanied by erections and a sensation of pleasure, at last become passive. After the spermatorrhœa, or without having been preceded by it, there occur after some months or years, progressive diminution of desire, difficulty in pro-

* Clinique Médicale de l'Hotel Dieu de Paris. Tome Deux., p. 534, et seq.

† De l'Ataxie Locomotrice et en particulier de la Maladie appelée Ataxie Locomotrice Progressive. Paris, 1864, p. 171.

curing satisfaction, and at last absolute impotence."

Eisenmann reports a case (Topinard) in which priapism existed thirty years. "During thirty years of his life, priapism had tormented this patient, and was only calmed by continually increasing and enormous doses of opium."

In order to exhibit the relation of the genital symptoms to the other phenomena in cases of progressive locomotor ataxia, I subjoin an analysis of the symptoms of the first period in the five cases of which I have preserved notes:

The disease commenced in No. 1, at 35. He is 5 feet 6 in. in height; has a light complexion, light auburn hair, blue eyes, and the lymphatic temperament. The first symptoms manifested themselves in No. 2, at 40 years of age; he is now 65. He is 5 feet 8 in. in height, of nervous temperament; has blue eyes, and his hair, now gray, was originally auburn. No. 3 experienced the first symptoms at 43; he is now 46. He has also a fair complexion, blue eyes, and light auburn hair. No. 4 was 42 years of age when he began to experience the pains; he is now 45. He is 5 feet 10 in. in height, and has a dark complexion, dark eyes and black hair. No. 5 experienced his first symptoms at 37, ten years ago. He has reddish hair and beard, blue eyes, and a strongly marked nervous temperament.

No. 1 had satyriasis, spermatorrhœa, tingling and numbness of the feet and legs, and amaurosis and double vision. The satyriasis was soon succeeded by anaphrodisia and impotence. The dimness of vision and the double vision suddenly disappeared at the commencement of the second period. He did not experience those peculiar pains so commonly present in this disease. The whole duration of the first period, commencing with the satyriasis, was only three months. The symptoms of the first period in No. 2 were similar in character, but extended over a much longer period. The state of the sexual appetite in the beginning could not be accurately ascertained, but anaphrodisia soon occurred, and absolute impotence was the final result. Violent pains, supposed to be rheumatic, preceded the other symptoms. These pains are localized in the inferior extremities, and especially in the left hip, so that disease of this articulation was suspected. No derangement of vision occurred at any period. No. 3 experienced, for more than a year, sharp pains in the extremities, and also deep-seated pains in the trunk, before the ataxia manifested itself. These pains, being sudden in onset, fugitive in character, and irregular in their recurrence, were supposed to be neuralgic. A decided decrease in sexual desire, and imperfect sexual congress were observed, but complete anaphrodisia did not occur. Dimness of sight, but no other ocular trouble, has thus far been present in this case. In No. 4, two years of neuralgic pains preceded the other symptoms. The pains had the two characters so frequently noticed in this disease: the first, deep-seated, dull, and heavy, pretty nearly constant; the second, sharp and sudden, temporary. The dull and heavy pains experienced in the lumbar region, in the thighs, and in certain parts of the trunk, preceded the others, which attacked the legs and thighs. No ocular derangement occurred in this case. Spermatorrhœa, anaphrodisia, and impotence, however, were experienced early. No. 5 began to have pains in the lumbar region in 1857, and soon after severe attacks of neuralgia along the course of the sciatic. These were succeeded by sharp, sudden, and fugitive pains in both inferior extremities.

The patient compares these pains to electric shocks. Anaphrodisia and spermatorrhœa did not occur until two years after the pains had been experienced. He admits that at the present time he is completely impotent. Derangements of vision manifested themselves in two years after the commencement of his malady. These consisted in amblyopia and double vision. They disappeared suddenly—in a night, he says—after continuing for several months.

After the first period has passed there can be no difficulty in coming to a conclusion as to the relation of the spermatorrhœa to the other phenomena.

Various other affections of the nervous system are accompanied by involuntary seminal losses. Diseases of the medulla, cerebellum and pons, of the spinal cord, epilepsy, chronic mania, may have this as a more or less pronounced symptom. In the early stage of diabetes, before impotence results, spermatorrhœa is sometimes present.

In all cases in which the involuntary loss is a symptom merely, it is of little consequence from the therapeutical point of view; the centric lesion, of which it is a sign, is the point of importance to which our attention should be directed.

III.

IMAGINARY SPERMATORRHŒA.

It is important to bear in mind that involuntary seminal losses, to constitute a disease, should occur with sufficient frequency to produce definite symptoms. Many patients who come to a physician for advice and treatment for this affection, are not really suffering from the seminal losses, but from an imaginary ailment. Experiencing an occasional seminal loss, and ignorant in regard to the physiological condition, they imagine themselves the subjects of spermatorrhœa. Brooding over their presumed "weakness," they fall into a hypochondriacal state, and soon experience the whole train of wretched symptoms depicted in popular works on the subject. Every subjective sensation, no matter what its origin, is referred to the debilitating effects of the spermal losses. As an evidence of the attention which these aptients give to their sensations, and of their mental and moral peculiarities, I subjoin a written statement handed to me by one of them, on presenting himself at my consultation-rooms:

"Ringing in my ears occasionally.

"Fulness and weight in stomach at all times.

"Considerable wind in the stomach.

"Want of strength in thighs and groins.

"Dull, heavy feeling in back of head at night and after dinner.

"Drowsiness after supper, so that I cannot read.

"Great want of clearness and want of strength of vision.

"Weakness of voice, and sometimes thickness of speech.

"Very sensitive to the least rudeness, and very apt to become nervous and low-spirited from being harassed or worried in any way.

"Heart palpitates somewhat violently at times.

"Digestion is very imperfect.

"Dryness of the scalp.

"Have been very subject to having boils on my legs, which always were of a dry nature.

"Apt to have pimples on forehead and neck."

All of these symptoms he referred to seminal emissions, occurring at intervals of three weeks. His health was robust, and he was actively engaged in business; but the corners of his mouth were depressed, and his countenance had an air of deep dejection.

Cases of this kind are very numerous, and difficult to manage. No explanation or demonstration satisfies them. One apprehension allayed, they quickly take up another, returning at last to the sexual disorder. They exhibit a real pleasure in dwelling upon this infirmity, and in talking with endless iteration over all the disgusting details connected with it.

Certain masturbators, struggling to free themselves from the trammels of the vice, but too weak of will to resist it wholly, please themselves with the delusion that the act is involuntary, because it is indulged in during the dreamy consciousness of the half-waking state. They consult the physician under the guise of having involuntary evacuations.

4

IV.

TREATMENT.

A CORRECT view of the pathology of spermatorrhœa is necessary to its successful curative treatment.

If spermatorrhœa be a purely local disease—an inflammation and ulceration of the prostatic portion of the urethra—local treatment only will be required. If, however, the essential condition consists of an increased reflex excitability of the spinal cord, due to frequent peripheral irritation seated in the urethra, then the local must be regarded as accessory to the general treatment. The relative importance of these two views as to the causation of the disease, should be definitely ascertained. A particular plan of treatment is followed by the adherents of each view. A wise therapeutist will not reject whatever is beneficial in either plan.

THE LOCAL TREATMENT consists in the application of the *porte caustique* to the prostatic portion of the urethra; the use of injections of the nitrate of silver, sulphate of copper, acetate of lead, etc.;

certain mechanical expedients; the internal administration of copaiba, cubebs, and other remedies of this class; cold hip-bathing, and injections of cold water into the rectum, etc. The most important of these measures is the use of the porte caustique. This instrument has been largely employed since its introduction for this purpose. Few practical surgeons at the present day will assent to the dictum of Lallemand, that "two-thirds of the cases of spermatorrhœa would be beyond the reach of medical assistance, if it were not for the good effects produced by the application of the nitrate of silver to the prostatic portion of the urethra."

It is very desirable, however, to ascertain its real importance and the limits of its application.

The Porte Caustique.—This instrument, which is so closely associated with the name of Lallemand, had an existence long anterior to his employment of it. Ambrose Paré devised an instrument for cauterizing the urethra, which is the progenitor of the modern instruments for this purpose. It consisted of a silver canula and a stylet of the same metal, having at its extremity a tampon of linen which was dusted with powdered caustic. Loizeau is said to have cured King Henry IV. of France of an induration of the urethra (organic structure) with a similar instrument. Wiseman, of England, and afterwards Hunter, employed the nitrate of silver in a porte caustique, but the latter substituted a caustique holder for the linen tampon. Sir Everard Home* was a warm advocate for the proceeding of Hunter. The instrument of Ducamp was the more immediate progenitor of Lallemand's. It was a *porte caustique* composed of a gum elastic canula, the stylet being an ordinary bougie, and of a caustic holder of platinum which was attached to the bougie. Amussat† in 1824 also invented a porte caustique, the canula being of silver, and the stylet, of the same metal, contained at its extremity a platinum point for lodging the caustic. About the same time Lallemand proposed his instrument, and a discussion arose

* Practical Observations on the Treatment of Strictures of the Urethra and Esophagus. Second Edition. London: 1797. P. 116 et seq.

† *Leçons du Amussat, sur les rétentions d'urine, etc.* Paris: 1831, p. 115 et seq., from which many of these particulars have been obtained.

as to the value of each instrument respectively. Differing in merely mechanical arrangements, the object to be attained in the use of them was essentially the same. The application of the caustic was employed in cases of thickening of the canal, ulceration and stricture due to chronic inflammation. We find in Lallemand's treatise on the disease of the genito-urinary organs,* the germ of those ideas put forth in full maturity fifteen years later in his work *Des pertes séminales involontaires.* After a discussion of the changes produced by blennorrhagia, he proceeds as follows:

"It may be easily conceived that irritation of the mucous membrane of the prostatic portion may extend itself to the ejaculatory canals, the vesiculæ seminales, etc.; and the proof is, the engorgement of the testicle which so frequently accompanies stricture. The results of this irritation of the seminal reservoirs and ejaculatory ducts are, that the act of coitus is promptly followed by the ejaculation; that the patients have

* *Observations sur les Maladies des Organes Génito-urinaires, Première Partie.* Paris: 1825, p. 158.

frequent nocturnal pollutions, and that in some cases the voluptuous sensation is accompanied by a more or less acute pain. Still further, the irritation augmenting, the seminal emission takes place with an incomplete erection, or is expelled with the last drops of urine. . . . . *Governed by analogy and by direct experiences, I have not hesitated to apply to these parts the nitrate of silver;* the mucous membrane takes on a new action; a benign inflammation supplants the chronic inflammation; tone is restored to the tissues, and the mucous secretion progressively diminishes." The original idea of Lallemand, following Paré, Hunter, Ducamp, and others, was the treatment of these chronic inflammatory affections of the urethra resulting in stricture, ulceration, and abscess. The extension of the method of cauterization to the treatment of spermatorrhœa was an after-thought. Very diverse views have obtained since as to the utility of the *porte caustique.* It has not, in general, produced that favorable impression upon these cases claimed for it by its advocates. Not only does it often fail to cure the patient, but the application of the caustic is frequently followed by most serious consequences.* In all cases it produces great irritation, frequently strangury and bloody urine, and sometimes severe urethritis and cystitis. Too long contact of the caustic may induce induration and organic stricture, a very serious complication of the case. Notwithstanding these sometimes unfortunate results, some surgeons adhere to it, and a few claim all that Ducamp, or Amussat, or Hunter, or Home, did in former times. Mr. Acton, for instance, is a zealous partisan of the porte caustique, contending [p. 225] that, as far as his own experience is concerned, it "fully bears out" the statement of Lallemand as to the infrequency of any ill consequences arising from its use. We should not, therefore, reject this practice of cauterization entirely. Under what circumstances may we resort to it? There appear to be two classes of cases in which it is indicated:

1st. Those in which chronic inflammatory changes exist as a complication of spermatorrhœa.

* Thompson, On Enlarged Prostate: Its Pathology and Treatment, etc. Op. cit.

2d. Those in which the moral effect of the application is desirable.

We have already, we think, conclusively established that the lesions of the prostatic portion of the urethra, described by Lallemand as constant to spermatorrhœa, are only accidental. They are produced by inflammation arising in the course of gonorrhœa, as appears evident enough indeed, on the perusal of the cases given by Lallemand in his treatise on diseases of the urinary organs. At all events, it is not at all common to find such changes in the urethra of patients suffering from seminal weakness in this country. A hyperæsthetic state of the canal, especially of the prostatic part, is, on the other hand, a most usual condition.

Romberg* has very well indicated the cases of the second class to which the use of the porte caustique is adapted: "Spermatorrhœa, to which not unfrequently hypochondriasis is to be attributed, requires special attention, and if all other remedies fail, we must have recourse to cauterization of the urethra, which has a *moral* as well

* Manual of the Nervous Diseases of Man. Op. cit. Vol. i., p. 188.

as a physical effect, by withdrawing the patient's attention from his malady." It is not improbable that to this "moral effect" is to be attributed much of whatever good is accomplished by the use of the porte caustique.

We would limit the application of caustic, then, to those conditions of inflammation, ulceration, and hyperæsthesia of the prostatic portion of the urethra, which proved refractory to other less painful and dangerous methods. For the moral effect, we would limit it to those obstinate cases accompanied with severe hypochondria, in which the fancy of the patient referred all the suffering to the region of the prostate, and to the cases of youths who persevered in the vice of masturbation.

The use of the porte caustique is not attended with difficulty. Certain precautions, however, are requisite to avoid injury to the parts. In the first place, it is necessary to ascertain the length of the canal, which may be done by introducing the catheter and observing the moment it enters the bladder. The length of the urethra from the meatus to the bladder is then marked on the canula. The curette is now charged with melted nitrate of silver and placed in the canula, which is oiled and introduced the desired length. The operator, however, will perceive when he enters the sphincter of the bladder by the sensation of the passage of the enlarged extremity of the instrument. Now when this enlarged extremity is withdrawn through the sphincter the sensation will be quite distinct, and the operator will know that he is in the prostatic part. It is only necessary to withdraw the outer canula half an inch and rotate rapidly the curette, withdrawing it quickly into the canula. Before the operation is performed the patient should empty the bladder, and he should not make water for some hours afterwards. The recumbent position should be enjoined, diluents and alkalies prescribed, and a moderate diet directed. Should there be much pain, opiates, morphia, or chlorodyne may be prescribed, or an anodyne suppository, or an enema of starch and laudanum may be introduced. For several days afterwards considerable irritation is experienced, even when most care has been exercised.

Injections.—If cauterization be desirable, it may be accomplished by injection. This is certainly as effectual and much safer than the preceding operation. A special instrument, such as Mr. Acton's glass syringe, may be employed, or the universal syringe (Fig. 3), which may be fitted to a silver catheter, will suffice for the purpose. The catheter must be introduced into the bladder, and then withdrawn into the prostatic portion of the urethra. The solution of nitrate of silver, of sulphate of copper, of acetate of lead, or, preferably, of tanno-glycerine (ʒ j.—℥ j.), may now be injected and allowed to apply itself thoroughly to the mucous surface. Not more than ʒ j of the solution should be used at a time, and too great force should be avoided lest the fluid be thrown into the bladder. The strength of the nitrate of silver solution should not exceed gr. x.—℥ j. Before the injection is made the patient should be required to empty the bladder, and should avoid emission of urine after as long as possible. Injections by an ordinary penis syringe are sometimes recommended, but they are entirely futile. It is difficult, if not impossible, to make efficient application in this way to the prostatic part of the urethra.

(Fig. 3.) (Fig. 4.)

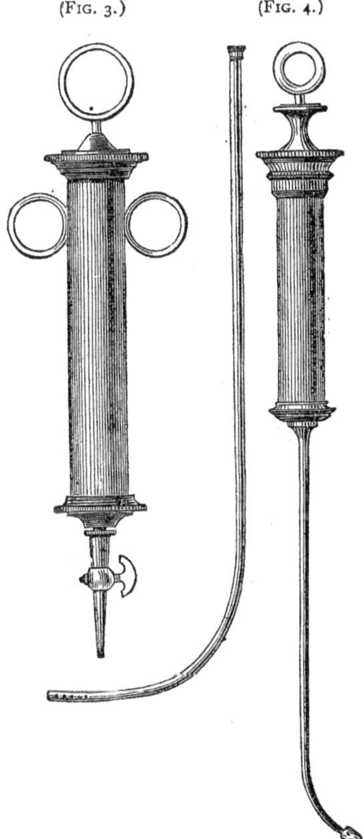

The instruments and appliances referred to in the text may be obtained from Mr. Wm. Autenreith, No. 71, West Sixth street, Cincinnati, Ohio.

A great many instruments have been devised for making application to the prostatic part of the urethra. It would be a waste of space to mention them all. The universal syringe and catheter answer most purposes. I have had constructed, in imitation of many that have been devised, a syringe which is very useful for this purpose. It consists of an ordinary hard-rubber syringe having a nozzle the diameter of a No. 6 catheter, and seven inches in length. The nozzle terminates by an olive-shaped blind extremity, behind which are a number of orifices for the escape of fluid. (Fig. 4.) The injected fluid flows from within outward, and is prevented by the bulb in front from escaping into the bladder.

Catheterism is beneficial in that state of hyperæsthesia of the prostatic part of the urethra which is so commonly present in cases of spermatorrhœa. The mere stretching of the canal by a full-sized bougie or catheter has the effect to diminish the excessive sensibility of the parts, and the moral effect of the introduction of the instrument is not inconsiderable.

Circumcision.—When the prepuce is long the *glans penis* is kept moist and the epithelial layer becomes exceedingly delicate and susceptible. The abundant sensitive nerves of the glans are thus placed in the most favorable condition for the reception of impressions; an irritation experienced there is promptly, and with heightened impulse, conveyed to the cord, and hence, in the act of coitus, the emission takes place too quickly. So too, in sleep, the venereal impulse takes its origin, frequently, in these nerves thus endowed with an exaggerated sensibility. For these reasons, the operation of circumcision is frequently necessary in the treatment of spermatorrhœa. It would, probably, be well for society if the Jewish rite were made universal. It is a well-known fact, that, although the Jews suffer from gonorrhœa, they are rarely affected with syphilis. My observation justifies me in asserting that it is uncommon to meet a Jew afflicted with "seminal weakness." The freedom with which they expose themselves to contagion, and their great sexual activity, would, certainly, favor the occurrence of these disorders, if circumcision did not prove a protection. A knowledge of this hygienic fact, probably, existed at a very remote period of antiquity, for, according to Herodotus,* the Egyptian priests "practised circumcision for cleanliness, considering it better to be cleanly than comely." The editor of Herodotus in a foot-note expresses the belief that "this institution reaches to the most remote antiquity; we find it existing more than 2,400 years before our era, and there is no reason to doubt that it dated still earlier." At first confined to the priests, it afterwards extended through all ranks of society, as the benefits of the practice became known. In all probability the Jews obtained it from the Egyptians.

Other instrumental methods.—We may classify under this head various mechanical appliances to prevent involuntary seminal discharges. A useful expedient of this kind is a leather ring armed with metallic points large enough to be worn without discomfort until erection occurs, when the pricking will arouse the patient. This instrument may be employed by those who have decided erections and the emission with a distinct orgasm. Trousseau † recommends the introduc-

* Vol. ii., chap. 37, p. 53.

† *Clinique Médicale de l'Hotel Dieu*, etc., op. cit., vol. ii., p. 646-8.

tion of a pear-shaped cylinder of wood into the rectum to compress the prostate and seminal ducts. This barbarous contrivance, as it seems to me, cannot prevent venereal excitement and erection, although it may prevent emission, or force the semen backward into the bladder. Trousseau, however, speaks warmly in its praise, and adduces evidences of the good effects of the practice. Any theoretical objection which we may entertain must yield to the demonstrations of clinical observation. Accordingly, I will, when a suitable case presents itself, give this method of treatment a fair trial. Meanwhile, having no experience of its use to narrate, we propose to put our readers in possession of the experience of M. Trousseau. He observes that this apparatus has been of real service, and that more than one case, rebellious under all methods of treatment, yielded completely and promptly to this means. He alludes especially to the rapid return of the virile power in the cases treated in this way.

In the same category may be classed the method of acupuncture. This consists in passing long needles into the prostate, vesiculæ seminales, and sometimes into the testes and vasa deferentia.

Lallemand thinks it unfortunate that acupuncture has fallen into disuse! We can hardly join in his regrets. A general objection may be urged against all of those mechanical appliances, that they fix the attention of the patient upon his infirmity, thereby retarding recovery.

Another remedy, proposed in Trousseau's clinical lecture on spermatorrhœa, is *forced dilatation of the anus.* This practice was recommended to him by Dr. Adolphe Richard, who operated on a case in Trousseau's presence, with a most fortunate result. Four months afterwards Dr. Richard received a letter from the young man, announcing that the good effects continued. The frequent passage of rectal bougies, increased to the utmost capacity of the anus, is, sometimes, very beneficial.

The internal medicines intended to act locally, are chiefly copaiba and cubebs. They need only be mentioned to be condemned, for the irritation which they produce in the mucous membrane of the stomach and kidney will more than counterbalance any possible good which they can accomplish in the urethra. Enemas of cold water and other medicaments and suppositories are capable of much more useful results. We have found urethral suppositories, especially, of great utility in those cases of so-called "diurnal pollutions," which consist essentially of urethral leucorrhœa.

THE MEDICAL TREATMENT has consisted in the main in efforts to improve the general health by appropriate tonics, as iron, quinine, strychnia, sea-bathing, douches, etc.; by suitable dietetics; by improved hygiene, etc. Conjoined with these measures anaphrodisiacs are employed as they seem to be indicated.

REMEDIES EMPLOYED IN THE TREATMENT OF SPERMATORRHŒA.—It will be convenient to discuss under this head the actions and uses of the most approved remedies.

Anaphrodisiacs.—One of the oldest of these remedies is camphor. *Camphora per nares castrat odore mares*, was an aphorism of the school of Salernum. It is not, however, a very valuable remedy. To produce the desired anaphrodisiac effect large doses are necessary; it frequently fails, and its action upon the stomach is unpleasant, giving rise to a sense of heat and burning, and followed by disagreeable eructations.

Lupulin is much employed by many distinguished therapeutists. Thus it is a favorite remedy with Lebert,* who gives it in combination with camphor. It has considerable efficacy as an anaphrodisiac, but, like camphor, it is uncertain. Belladonna, or better its alkaloid, atropia, is much more efficient than camphor. Our indigenous remedy, *gelsemium*, is still more powerful in its action on the sexual organs. The fluid extract of either of these agents may be combined with other anaphrodisiacs, or they may be given alone. The tincture of belladonna and the tincture of gelsemium may be prescribed with advantage together.

The most important agent of this class, the most efficient and certain, and the least distressing in its immediate and remote effects, when freely administered, is the bromide of potassium. The anaphrodisiac property of this drug is now almost universally acknowledged, but the conditions of its success and failure have not been as definitely determined as is desirable. There are yet some

* Op. cit., vol. ii. p. 587.

sceptics who disbelieve in this property of the bromide of potassium. One of the most recent and pretentious of them is Dr. S. W. Duckworth Williams.* The cases submitted by him in proof of his views serve very well to illustrate the conditions under which the bromide of potassium fails to produce its characteristic effects. We accordingly reproduce them in Dr. Williams's words, as they are very suitable to our purpose. "Dr. Crichton Browne, in a pamphlet on 'The Action of the Bromide of Potassium upon the Nervous System,' published since I commenced writing these remarks, is very much inclined to allow it strong anaphrodisiac properties, although I cannot quite perceive on what data. He owns that he had had no opportunity of trying the bromide of potassium in simple nymphomania, although he used it without effect in one patient who was in a state of mania, following upon melancholia, and in whom there was presumed to be excitement of the sexual feelings, on account of the extraordinary obscenity of language which

* On the Efficacy of the Bromide of Potassium in Epilepsy and certain Psychical Affections. Churchill, London, 1865. (Pamphlet.)

she used. Now, I have tried it in every variety of uterine affection that has come within my reach, including nymphomania, satyriasis, menorrhagia, amenorrhœa, dysmenorrhœa, etc., etc., but without perceiving the least benefit accrue. . . . . I had under treatment at one time two cases that seemed especially well adapted for favoring the anaphrodisiac properties of this medicine. They were both strong, healthy girls, the one a lady, the other a domestic servant. Both were admitted into the asylum at Northampton, suffering from simple mania without any positive delusion. They were lively, excitable, restless, and extremely volatile, often able to command their faculties sufficiently to converse calmly and rationally for a few minutes on any ordinary subject, but liable at any moment to burst out laughing or into a fit of tears without any visible cause, or to begin to rave and scream, or swear; both were fine, handsome, fully developed young women; both were most indecent in language, voice, and gesture, and both openly practised self-pollution. The bromide of potassium was given to them in doses of gr. v. *bis die* in a little pure water, and increased up to gr. xx., and although both were much affected by its use, and both became pale and thin, and reduced, and their circulation powerfully controlled (indeed, in one case the pulsations were reduced from 90 to 60 beats in a minute), nevertheless they persisted in their bad habits, and their sensuality became, if possible, more confirmed. The administration of the medicine was persisted in for nearly twelve months in both cases.

"Another case in which I tried it was that of a married lady, nearly 40 years of age, in a state of chronic mania, and at the same time I made some observations as to the influence of the bromide on the heart's action. This lady was extremely amative, fell in love with every person of the opposite sex she encountered, and was in the habit of writing the most obscene letters to all her male acquaintances. Her pulse was habitually about 90—tolerably strong and full. Being of a strong constitution, I commenced by giving gr. xv. *bis die.* About an hour after the third dose her pulse was 76; two hours from that time it had almost regained its accustomed frequency, but in an hour's time from the fourth dose it was reduced to 70, and on one occasion during the first week it was nearly as low as 60. Combined with this decrease in the circulation there was, as might be expected, marked languor and ennui almost amounting to debility, and she seemed inclined to maintain the recumbent position constantly; but I cannot say that her lascivious wishes or ideas were in the least disturbed, or that her advances were marked by more delicacy; *au contraire*, I am not quite sure that she was not worse."

The experience of Dr. Williams, which seems so entirely opposed to that of other observers, is easily interpreted by a knowledge of the conditions which retard or altogether prevent the action of the bromide of potassium. In some investigations, published recently,* I attempted to define these conditions. My conclusions were embodied in the following:

"Its physiological effects are not very decided, and are readily modified by any local disturbance.

"Its therapeutical action is still more decidedly influenced by local morbid processes.

* Experimental Investigations into the Actions and Uses of the Bromide of Potassium. Cincinnati Lancet and Observer, 1865.

"It is indicated where a sedative to the nervous system is required, e. g.—in insomnia; too great reflex excitability; nervous and spasmodic affections of the larynx and bronchi; sexual excitement, and in an irritable state of the sexual organs.

"*It will be effectual in the foregoing conditions, in proportion to the degree in which structural lesions are absent, or in other words, in proportion to the degree in which these morbid states are functional rather than organic.*"

These conclusions, the result of observation and experiment, afford us a satisfactory solution of the cause of failure in the use of the bromide of potassium in cases such as those described by Dr. Williams. The cases of sexual excitement in mania are due, as is shown by Schroeder van der Kolk, to structural alteration in the medulla oblongata, the centre, according to this author, of the sexual impulse. The bromide of potassium can have no influence over these structural alterations, and hence cannot control the manifestations of sexual excitement which depend upon them.

Aphrodisiacs.—These are indicated under certain circumstances. The tincture of cantharides is sometimes beneficial in cases of great atony and relaxation—those characterized by profuse mucous discharge, so-called diurnal pollutions, very feeble power of erection, and absence of sexual desire. It is contra-indicated where much hyperæsthesia of the prostatic portion of the urethra exists. To prevent its irritant effects, or at least to reduce them to the minimum, opium, or cannabis indica, or chlorodyne, may be advantageously combined with it. The red or amorphous phosphorus, or phosphide of zinc, may be given in the same class of cases as suggested for the tincture of cantharides. Nux vomica is adapted to those cases in which it is desired to restore the functional activity of the sexual organs, after the state of quiescence induced by the prolonged administration of anaphrodisiacs. Cimicifuga (actea racemosa) has seemed to me to possess considerable aphrodisiac power, and has proved useful in cases of long-standing spermatorrhœa accompanied by nervousness and anxiety, and diminished sexual desire.

Galvanism, especially the induction current, and static electricity, are often decidedly aphrodisiac, and are probably applicable to more numerous cases than any other remedy of the class.

Duchenne* (de Boulogne) operates in the following manner: One rhéophore properly insulated is introduced into the rectum, and placed in contact with the *bas fond* of the bladder; the other is passed to the prostatic part of the urethra. In this way a current can be made to traverse the *vesiculæ seminales* and ejaculatory apparatus. Benedikt† applies "the copper pole to the lumbar vertebræ, and passes the zinc pole along the spermatic cords, over the different zones, transversely, of the penis, and along the perinæal region antero-posteriorly. . . Beside this, usually three times in two weeks, the copper pole is applied by means of a catheter-shaped rhéophore to the orifices of the ejaculatory ducts, and the zinc pole is passed along the spermatic cords."

Ergot has been much extolled in those cases in which emission takes place quickly with feeble erections.

Tonics.—Iron, quinine, the vegetable bitters, the mineral acids, are indicated in anæmic cases. The *hygienica*, air, exercise, bathing, travel, etc., are valuable adjuncts to the remedial measures.

* De l'Électrization Localisée. Paris, 1861, p. 97.
† Elektrotherapie. Wien, 1868, p. 446.

The Therapeutical Management of Spermatorrhœa comprehends—

First, the treatment of the causes.

Second, the treatment of the malady.

The Treatment of the Causes.—We have already expressed the opinion that venereal excesses, and especially masturbation, are the causes of spermatorrhœa, in a vast majority of cases as they occur in this country. Hence it is important to recognize this vice at an early period, to prevent the immediate and remote consequences of its continued perpetration.

We have already seen that this vice is contracted chiefly by boys in whom the nervous preponderates over the muscular and digestive systems, and that certain moral and social circumstances, and organic peculiarities, increase the tendency to it. These influences must, as far as possible, be repressed. Of course, it is not within the power of the physician to alter those inherent mental and physical defects which exercise such a baneful influence; but much may be done to diminish the activity of the nervous system, and to restore the balance between it and the other systems. Therefore, to the physical culture of boys possessing these inherited peculiarities too great importance cannot be attached. The development of the muscular and digestive systems should be promoted by every agency. Open air exercise, constant physical employment, avoidance of confinement and idleness, cold bathing, etc., are the means necessary for this purpose. Lebert * places chief reliance upon these hygienic means in all cases of masturbation and spermatorrhœa. The principal organic peculiarity promotive of this vice, is phymosis. Where this condition exists, the operation of circumcision is proper. A long and contracted prepuce hinders the development of the penis, and by retaining the moisture and secretions of the part, increases the sensibility of the glans.

Ignorance of the character and tendency of the habit favors the perpetration of masturbation. Parents and public teachers have a sad duty to perform in this connection which they naturally shrink from. In a large majority of cases, the habit would be discontinued, if the dreadful consequences of it were plainly set forth to the

* Op. cit., p. 784, vol. ii.

unfortunate victims. This becomes especially necessary in boarding schools and in other public institutions where numbers of boys are congregated.

It is also very important to prevent suggestive novels, and books of every description having a tendency to excite erotic ideas, falling into the hands of these youths.

As a general rule it is sufficient in cases of masturbation to set forth clearly the dangers of the practice; to institute a thorough system of physical culture; to reduce the mental work; to keep the body occupied; to correct, if possible, any organic imperfection which may be remedied (phymosis), in order to effect a cure. In some inveterate cases this may not be sufficient. The habit may be so confirmed, the instincts so low, and the moral obliquity so great, that no means other than physical restraint will prevent the perpetration of the act. The mechanical appliances may be assisted by anaphrodisiacs.

Mr. Heckford* has recently published a paper showing the great value of "circumcision as a

* London Hospital Reports, 1865, vol. ii., p. 62. Already quoted.

remedial measure in certain forms of epilepsy, chorea, etc." In the very instructive cases given by Mr. Heckford, the convulsive affections depended upon masturbation.

As the operation of circumcision is easily performed, and is without danger to life, it should not be omitted from the treatment in two classes of cases: 1. Those in which the habit of masturbation is due to the hyperæsthesia of the glans produced by an elongated prepuce and the irritation of the retained sebaceous matter; and 2. In those cases in which the same cause (a peripheral irritation) induces the venereal orgasm and involuntary discharge.

Although we do not deny the possibility of it, we regard it as rather improbable that a mere peripheral irritation, such as an irritable or inflamed state of the prostatic portion of the urethra, or a balanitis, will of itself produce the reflex phenomena of spermatorrhœa. Such irritation, however, will undoubtedly increase the morbid excitability of the reflex faculty, if it have already been aroused by such causes as masturbation and venereal excesses.

Ceasing an ill habit may suffice in many cases

to cure these local irritations. The operation of circumcision should be performed when the prepuce is long, the glans moist, and epithelium very sensitive. The frequent application of cold water to the glans, when in this condition, is of great service. The tanno-glycerine (ʒ i.—℥ i.) may also be applied daily to the glans with advantage. Similar measures may be adopted for an irritation in the prostatic part of the urethra: daily injections of cold water; the injection through a silver catheter in the manner already recommended, of the tanno-glycerine, or of a solution of nitrate of silver. But the irritable state of the prostatic portion is more properly an effect rather than a cause of spermatorrhœa; accordingly we postpone the further consideration of it until we come to treat of the therapeutic measures proper to the malady itself.

Remedial Management.—Remedies should be employed with reference to the pathological states of the several phases of spermatorrhœa.

In the genital form there are associated with the peripheral irritation increased reflex excitability and derangement of the primary assimilation. There may be a condition of plethora, or more or less emaciation; much more usually, the latter: the therapeutical methods are indicated in this brief pathological summary. In those rather exceptional cases, in which the spermatorrhœa is the result of plethora and forced continence, it may only be necessary to impart to the patient correct views of the importance of the losses, which, influenced by current publications, he will be very apt to exaggerate. If his vessels are full, his bowels are constipated, and his digestion active, he will be benefited, if somewhat reduced by saline cathartics, by *liquor potassæ*, by a less liberal diet, by abundant exercise, and by diminishing the number of hours devoted to sleep. Many cases of so-called idiopathic spermatorrhœa occur in studious persons of sedentary habits, whose nervous system has been rendered unduly excitable by prolonged mental work with enfeebled digestive powers. These are relieved by mental rest, by some physical employment, and by attention to the state of the digestive organs.

Activity of the sexual system may be associated with this excitable state of the nervous system in studious persons; when, of course, the anaphrodisiac remedies will be required. It has happened to me to meet cases of this character in clergymen who led a life of celibacy. A judicious employment of the hygienic means together with the medical, and especially a candid statement of the real importance of the infirmity, will be followed by most satisfactory results.

A vast majority of the patients who present themselves for treatment do not belong to either of the foregoing classes. They are those in whom seminal weakness has been induced by masturbation, or by prolonged excesses in venery. They have frequent nocturnal emissions. The reflex excitability of the cord is so much increased, that the feeblest irritation procures a prompt emission with little of the venereal orgasm, and the frequent discharges of nervous force affect the supply to all the organs—whence come palpitation, indigestion, constipation, irritable bladder, pain in the back, mental feebleness, and debility. The peripheral irritation and the reflex excitability must be diminished. These important objects may be accomplished by means partly hygienical and partly medicinal.

The patient should cease his excesses, whatever they may have been, and avoid all sources of excitement, whether the reading improper publications, suggestive novels or works upon his own malady, or the society of women of easy virtue. The liberties between the sexes permitted by custom in many places and in certain circles of society without extending so far as the gratification of desire, are so very injurious to young men with "seminal weakness," that they should be absolutely interdicted. The mind of the patient should be freed, as far as possible, from any association with his disagreeable infirmity. Hence constant and agreeable employment, physical rather than mental, or an association of the two, is especially desirable. The bromide of potassium will powerfully contribute to the success of these measures. Forty to sixty grains may be given every night until sexual desire is entirely suspended. This remedy has a decided power to allay urethral irritation, as we have found, not only in the cases for which it is now recommended, but in gonorrhœa after the acute stage has subsided, and in gleet. We observe that Mr. Hutchison * has committed himself to the same opinion. In that very distressing com-

* London Hospital Reports, vol. ii., p. 340.

plication of spermatorrhœa—hyperæsthesia of the spermatic plexus—the bromide of potassium is, also, very effective. If decided anæmia exist in these cases of the genital form, iron and quinia may be given during the day, conjoined with lupulin, should it be desirable to increase the anaphrodisia.

We have seen that dilatation of the inter-rachidian vessels probably exists in advanced cases. This view seems confirmed by the fact that the involuntary emissions occur much more certainly when the patient is lying on his back—a position favoring congestion of the cord. Hence management of the position in bed is not to be neglected. The patient should lie upon his side, and if unable to continue in this position when asleep, should adopt some mechanical appliances to compel it. Tying the hand to the bed-post so that the position of the back cannot readily be assumed may suffice in some instances. Or, Lallemand's contrivance may be adopted: this consists of a thin sheet of lead to which a piece of wood is fastened, attached by a girdle to the loins. Or, Mr. Acton's expedient, which is nothing more than a towel tied about the waist with a large knot behind. Or, lastly, the leather ring armed with metallic points, which will arouse the patient when erection occurs.

The principal remedial agent for inducing contraction of the inter-rachidian vessels is ergot. The drug should be fresh, or carefully prepared ergotin or fluid extract should be used. Gelsemium may be used for the same purpose. It is probably more effective even than ergot. Cold to the spine, not too prolonged, or alternate hot and cold douches, may be usefully conjoined with the ergot. It should be remembered, however, that cold to the spine is a powerful aphrodisiac.

If the patient experience the tenacious discharge from the urethra, consisting of the secretion from the prostate, Cowper's glands, and follicles of the mucous membrane, he will undoubtedly believe himself to have "diurnal pollutions," and will be correspondingly alarmed. If the discharge do not cease during the course of treatment just recommended, it will be necessary to adopt some special means to arrest it. These special means consist in the local application in the manner already indicated of tanno-glycerine, of solutions of nitrate of silver, or the use of the *porte caustique*. We should not forget, however, that caustic applications are considered by Henry Thompson * as a cause of prostatitis.

Our duty is not ended in a case of spermatorrhœa, with the production of a state of anaphrodisia and the curing of irritation in the urethra. We must restore the patient to the proper performance of his sexual functions, and this must be accomplished in such a way that he will not lapse into his former infirmity. The bromide of potassium and the ergot must be suspended, and tonics and special excitants must be employed. Extract of nux vomica or strychnia with iron, is a useful combination under these circumstances. Cimicifuga and gelsemium are also indicated, if there be any decided nervous phenomena present as a complication. Galvanism should not be neglected. In these cases, Duchenne's method should be practised: i.e., one rhéophore in the rectum ; the other passed into the prostatic part of the urethra. Benedikt reports great success by his mode of applying the

* On Enlarged Prostate : Its Pathology and Treatment. London, 1858, p. 195, op. cit.

currents. Sometimes static electricity is of great service. The patient is placed on an insulated stool, in communication with the prime conductor, and sparks are drawn from the genitals.

During the whole period occupied by this treatment certain accessories must not be disregarded. Simple but nutritious food must be taken; the supper should be light, and eaten four or five hours before retiring, and alcoholic stimulants should be avoided. The habitual use of tea, coffee, and tobacco should be discouraged. Fluids and articles of food having a diuretic action should be sparingly used, since erections occur when the bladder becomes full. Laxatives are indicated if constipation exist, but not otherwise.

In that phase of spermatorrhœa which we have denominated the cerebral, in addition to the derangement of the sexual-spinal system there exists some form of cerebral disorder. If the sexual troubles are mere symptoms of mental derangement, the treatment of them is merged into that for insanity. If, on the other hand, the mental derangement is the result of seminal losses or abuse, the treatment of it becomes associated necessarily with that for the cause. The cases given in the extract from Dr. Williams's pamphlet belong to the first class; the typical cases presented under the head of the cerebral form are instances of the second. The first are not amenable to the action of anaphrodisiacs, whilst the second are. Usually the mental derangement has proceeded no further than hypochondria, melancholia, or trembling delirium (delusional insanity) corresponding to delirium tremens of alcoholismus. In all of the psychical affections of spermatorrhœa, the bromide of potassium is very efficacious. Ergot shonld be administered in conjunction with it, and counter-irritants (firing, setons, blisters) should be applied to the nape of the neck, on Schroeder Van Der Kolk's plan, and also as recommended by Romberg.

The early recognition of mental disorders arising from abuse is very important. With the anaphrodisiacs—bromide of potassium, lupulin, and camphor—and moral agencies, should be conjoined the operation of circumcision. Physical constraint may also be resorted to, but this is a temporary expedient which more usually fails than succeeds. Division of the *vasa deferentia* in inveterate cases has been recommended, and we have seen it performed in an inveterate case. Nothing but a failure in the means already proposed will justify the performance of this operations, as in its practical results it is equivalent to castration. The operation is readily enough performed. The duct can be easily felt and separated from the rest of the spermatic cord, when it may be divided by the subcutaneous section.

In the spinal form of spermatorrhœa the treatment will be influenced by the condition of the cord. If the loss of power, the altered and referred sensations, the paraplegia, be merely functional derangements, or due to a "dynamic alteration," strychnia, cimicifuga, faradization, douches, hot and cold, to the spinal column, will be indicated. Bromide of potassium is hurtful in the paraplegia of sexual excess. It is, however, especially applicable to the treatment of the epilepsy and chorea of spermatorrhœa. The striking results obtained by Mr. Heckford, and my own observations, warrant, me in strongly urging the operation of circumcision, in those convulsive disorders due to masturbation. In the typical cases of the spinal form narrated under that head, I found the extract of belladonna of signal advantage.

Treatment of Impotence.—The temporary impotence of spermatorrhœa requires time and familiarity with the object of desire. If it consist of nothing more than such a degree of excitability of the reflex faculty, that intromission cannot be accomplished, or that the seminal discharge takes place after very imperfect coitus, then the treatment recommended for the genital form of spermatorrhœa may be pursued.

In the impotence dependent upon spermatorrhœa of long standing, hot and cold douches to the spine, galvanism or static electricity, and a properly conducted system of physical training and exercise, are the most appropriate measures. Special excitants may be employed in conjunction with these means: strychnia, phosphide of zinc, cannabis indica, cantharides, etc.; but these remedies will not be successful unless the general health has been restored by proper hygiene and suitable hæmatinics. When the impotence depends upon "irritable testis," a judicious course of bromide of potassium should precede the use of the other measures. Some of these cases may be very quickly cured by an induction current passed through an insulated metallic sound introduced into the bladder. The occasional passage of a full-sized catheter, I have found in not a few instances, to produce energetic erections.

The question of the propriety of marriage often involves considerations of great delicacy. Many cases are undoubtedly curable in this way. Marriage will always have a fortunate result in the cases of spermatorrhœa of physiological origin. In true spermatorrhœa, marriage may be enjoined when the genital apparatus is not so impaired in function as to prevent intromission. Regular intercourse, not too frequently repeated, will prove of signal advantage in these cases. At first sexual contact may be unsatisfactory in consequence of the greatly increased reflex excitability of the ejaculatory apparatus; but power increases by judicious use of the organs.

Singular as the opinion may appear, I cannot refrain from stating that marriage has resulted unhappily more frequently in cases of imaginary spermatorrhœa than in the other forms described. When the supposed existence of this trouble becomes a predominant idea, and moral and medicinal treatment cannot destroy or weaken it, marriage will only confirm the delusion, for the first attempts proving failures, the patient will give himself up to the most absolute conviction of incompetence.

FORMULÆ.

INJECTIONS.

℞.

Argenti Nitrat., gr. x.
Aquæ Distil., ℥j.
Solve.

℞.

Zinc. Sulphat., gr. xij.
Morphiæ Sulphat., gr. iv.
Atropiæ Sulphat., gr. ss.
Aquæ Distil., ℥j.
M.

℞.

Acidi Tannici, ʒj.
Glycerini, ℥j.
M.

℞.

Acid. Tannici, ʒj.
Tinct. Iodinii, ʒss.
Glycerini, ℥j.
M.

Anaphrodisiacs.

℞.

Lupulin., gr. vj.
Pulv. Camphoræ, gr. iij.
Ext. Belladonnæ, gr. j.
ft. pil. No. vi.
S. One 3 times a day.

℞.

Atropiæ Sulphat., gr. ss.
Aquæ Distil., ℥ ss.
M.
S. 3 to 5 drops 3 times a day.

℞.

Tinct. Gelsemii, ʒ j.
Tinct. Belladonnæ, ʒ ij.
M.
S. 15 drops 3 times a day.

℞.

Tinct. Gelsemii, ʒ j.
Tinct. Cimicifugæ, ʒ vij.
M.
S. 30 drops to a teaspoonful 3 times a day.

℞.

Potassii Bromidi, ℥ j.

ft. pulv. No. viii.

S. One dissolved in water every night.

℞.

Potassii Bromidi, ℥ j.

Ext. Gelsemii Fl. ʒ ij,

Syrp. Simpl. ℥ i.

Aquæ Cinnamomi, ℥ iij.

M.

S. A teaspoonful 3 times a day.

℞. Potassii Bromidi, ℥ j.

Ext. Belladonnæ Fl.

Ext. Gelsemii Fl. āā ʒ ij.

Syrp. Simpl., ℥ iss.

Aquæ Menth. P., ℥ ij.

M.

S. A teaspoonful 3 times a day.

Aphrodisiacs.

℞.

Tinct. Cantharidis, ʒ j.

Tinct. Cannabis Ind.

Sol. Morphiæ Bi-mec., āā ℨ ij.
M.
S. 15 drops 3 times a day.

℞.
Zinci Phosphidi, gr. iij.
Conserv. Rosæ, ℨ ss.
ft. pil. no. xxx.
S. One night and morning.

℞.
Tinct. Nucis Vom., ℨ j.
Tinct. Acteæ Rac., ℨ iij.
M.
S. 20 drops 3 times a day.

℞.
Syrp. Ferri, Quiniæ, et Strychniæ Phos., ℥ ij.
S. A teaspoonful 3 times a day.

℞.
Auri Terchloridi, gr. j.
Ext. Nucis Vom., gr. v.
ft. pil. No. xx.
S. One 3 times a day.

Urethral Suppositories.

℞.

Iodoformi,
Acid. Tannici, āā, gr. vj.
Ol. Theobrom., q. s.
ft. supposit. ureth. no. vi.

℞.

Acid. Tannici, gr. vj.
Ex. Belladonnæ, gr. j.
Ol. Theobrom., q. s.
ft. supposit. ureth. no. vi.

℞.

Plumbi Acetat., gr. xij.
Morphiæ Acetat., gr. j.
Ol. Theobrom., q. s.
ft. supposit. ureth. no. vi.

℞.

Morphiæ Sulph., gr. iij.
Zinci Sulph., gr. vj.
Ol. Theobrom., q. s.
ft. supposit. ureth. no. vi.

THE END.

www.ingramcontent.com/pod-product-compliance
Lightning Source LLC
LaVergne TN
LVHW010743120826
845150LV00009B/1976

* 9 7 8 1 4 2 5 5 0 9 5 6 9 *